Ancient Practices *for* Mindful Living

Ancient Practices *for* Mindful Living

AATMANIKA RAM

HAY HOUSE

HAY HOUSE INDIA

New Delhi • London • Sydney

Carlsbad, California • New York City

Hay House Publishers (India) Pvt Ltd
Muskaan Complex, Plot No. 3, B-2, Vasant Kunj, New Delhi – 110070, India

Hay House LLC, P.O. Box 5100, Carlsbad, CA 92018-5100, USA
Hay House UK Ltd, 1st Floor, Crawford Corner, 91-93 Baker Street, London W1U 6QQ, UK
Hay House Australia Publishing Pty Ltd, 18/36 Ralph St., Alexandria NSW 2015, Australia

Email: contact@hayhouse.co.in
Website: www.hayhouse.co.in

First published by Hay House India, 2024
10 9 8 7 6 5 4 3 2 1

ISBN 978-81-97328-51-0
ISBN 978-81-97328-54-1 (E-Book)

Printed at Replika Press Pvt Ltd

MIX
Paper | Supporting responsible forestry
FSC™ C016779
FSC www.fsc.org

Hay House is committed to a sustainable future for our business, our readers and our planet. This book is made from Forest Stewardship Council® certified paper.

To my perfectly imperfect inner child,
'You are enough, I am enough. All those daughters who come after me, are enough.'

Contents

Foreword

It is a privilege to write the foreword for this book authored by a good friend whom I have known for over three decades. Aatmanika is one of the most genuine people I know. I am delighted that this dynamic lady of multifarious talents has chosen to share her learnings and journey of mindfulness through these pages, for I admire the grace with which she has thus far navigated life, living up to the challenges of being a global citizen, moving through multiple countries, all the while cherishing and celebrating her womanhood and her Indianness. The deep inner reflections that she engages in when faced with life's innumerable anomalies and dichotomies, while she continues to give generously of herself to her family, colleagues, friends, and relatives who are spread across continents, unveil the strength of this connoisseur of life. The conscious efforts that she puts into attaining mastery in whatever she does, be it conjuring up elaborate, delicious, exotic meals, tending to the plants in her garden, or writing insightful blogs and articles, are all an expression of the unique and caring way in which Aatmanika celebrates life itself, polishing all she does to a fine art.

Through her mindfulness journey, I have watched her blossom as she learnt to take one day at a time, learning to stay in the now, as she continued to face the myriad challenges life throws at one spiritedly. Her explorations into herself made her listen to her physical body by practising yoga, going on long, mindful walks to rejuvenate in the lap of nature, of which we are all a part, and developing mindful eating. Along this journey, she listened to experts who have been on the path before and read extensively, choosing with discernment the choicest books on mindfulness to spur her along deeper on the path. The freedom from guilt and from being one's own worst critic is something most human beings crave. I have observed her grow immensely in her capacity to accept and love herself, learning to deeply cherish being itself and moving away from the self-doubt that we all experience at some point. Aatmanika is certainly a person who has seen success in this and is sailing smoothly along in acknowledging her inner richness and fulfilment. That she has now chosen to pen her experiences and success in reclaiming the ever-fresh youthfulness and joy that I have known to characterise her is indeed reflective of her integrity and magnanimous nature.

This book, an original read that one may savour slowly with intentional focus—allowing oneself to be immersed and revel in the abundance that is life itself—is bound to be counted amongst those that are written to fulfil the natural yearning of a human heart to share the rediscovery of its inherent joy and wisdom generously.

—Dr Gayathri Deepak
Founder and Director, Chetana Education

Why Yet Another Book on Mindfulness?

In a world where mindfulness literature seems to be multiplying faster than thoughts in a restless mind, one might wonder: Why add another drop to the ocean of mindfulness books?

Picture this—shelves sagging under the weight of countless books promising inner peace, serenity, and a Zen-like existence. Amidst the cacophony of mindfulness books, each author has a unique motive for penning their thoughts. With so many choices, how does one decide what to read?

Let us dive into the reasons behind the compulsion to write yet another book on this ancient practice that seems to have a modern-day renaissance.

How Is This Book Different?

Understanding the intentions behind writing a new book can shed light on what sets it apart from the rest. The author intends to offer readers a fresh and distinctive perspective on mindfulness that they may not have encountered before. She also aspires to share personal experiences, challenges, and triumphs in a way that brings immense value to readers and positively impacts their lives.

Throughout the author's life, there have been moments where embracing mindfulness was not merely a choice but a necessity. The author recounts several instances when she had to practise mindfulness to not only improve her mental health but as a vital form of survival as well.

Many of us seek books that offer solutions to our problems. In this narrative, the author recounts how mindfulness has helped regulate emotions daily, hoping readers can benefit from these insights and apply them to their own lives. Whether it is finding solutions to common issues, gaining new knowledge and wisdom, or embarking on an emotional journey, the genuine desire is for readers to deeply connect with the author's odyssey and discover the inherent value of this book. After all, no other book would have her story.

How Would the Book Resonate with the Reader?

In a sea of theories and practices, personal narratives act as lighthouses guiding readers through the turbulent waters of mindfulness literature. These stories inspire and offer a relatable human touch to an often-abstract subject. Books based on personal experiences feel more believable since research indicates that readers perceive information as more trustworthy when it stems from an individual's firsthand comprehension.

Authenticity is the currency of mindfulness literature. Through personal mindfulness journeys, readers can witness the struggles, triumphs, and moments of clarity that make the practice tangible and real. It is not just about mindfulness but how it feels to embody it in everyday life.

Mindfulness and other abstract concepts become more meaningful when they are relatable to the reader's personal experiences.

What Information Do the Chapters in This Book Provide?

In a world filled with picture-perfect Instagram yogis and Zen masters, the author has tapped on her vulnerability to share her imperfect and messy mindfulness journey. The author bravely bares her soul by sharing her personal experiences and draws upon her extensive expertise to provide practical insights and actionable recommendations for those looking to enhance their skills and stay ahead of the curve.

The chapters that follow in this book not only contain information on the methods that have been proven to be effective in various contexts in the author's journey but also explore the underlying principles and theories that support these methods. Each chapter is designed to equip readers with the knowledge and tools they need to succeed in today's competitive landscape on both personal and professional levels.

No two mindfulness journeys are alike, much like no two sunsets paint the sky in the same hues. By sharing unique experiences and learnings from personal mindfulness practices, the author illuminates the multifaceted nature of mindfulness and its transformative potential.

How Can This Book on Mindfulness Contribute to My Growth?

Before delving into the potential benefits of this book, it would be helpful for the readers to engage in introspection to determine the type of personal growth they seek. Regardless of the kind of growth one pursues—personal, professional, emotional, or physical—it is important to recognise that they are all interconnected and play a significant role in one's overall well-being. Understanding the interconnectedness of these different aspects of growth can lead to a more holistic approach to self-improvement and a greater sense of fulfilment in life.

This book serves as a vital resource for personal development, offering valuable insights into how mindfulness can drive personal success and positively influence one's professional life. The author guides readers through her journey of utilising mindfulness techniques to address issues proactively and develop a state of preparedness to handle adversities that may arise.

The author and her husband are dedicated practitioners of mindfulness, committed to personal growth and achieving success in both their professional pursuits and personal lives. Success, while subjective, becomes within reach for individuals striving for excellence in all their endeavours. This book provides a roadmap for those seeking to enhance their personal and professional lives through the power of mindfulness.

Self-awareness of emotions and attention to physical health is essential for addressing potential issues stemming from poor health and emotions. This heightened self-awareness enables better control over one's actions and behaviours not just personally but also in the workplace, leading to improved communication and conflict resolution with colleagues.

Professionals in various fields, including business, education, healthcare, and sports, have successfully integrated mindfulness practices into their routines to enhance focus, creativity, performance, and communication skills. Celebrities such as Oprah Winfrey, Kobe Bryant, and Beyoncé Knowles are known to practise meditation to centre their thoughts and emotions, highlighting the benefits of mindfulness in achieving personal and professional success.

My Attention Span Is Short. Can This Book Help?

The book provides strategies for managing stress and reducing mental clutter, further enhancing one's ability to sustain attention. In the following chapters, the author suggests ways to free oneself from feeling overwhelmed by mental clutter.

Mindfulness practices like meditation, deep breathing exercises, and body scans can help individuals develop the ability to stay engaged in the present moment without getting easily distracted. By implementing these techniques regularly, individuals can train their minds to concentrate on tasks for longer periods and improve their overall attention span.

Is Mindfulness Only for Those Dealing with Depression?

Contrary to popular belief, mindfulness is not solely reserved for individuals dealing with depression or adversity. It is important to first distinguish between feelings of depression and stress.

Stress is a temporary response to a challenging situation, typically marked by anxiety, tension, irritability, or decreased functioning.

Depression, on the other hand, is a more enduring mood disorder that can result from ongoing stressors and can be influenced by a variety of factors, including genetics, biology, environment, and psychology.

While stress can usually be managed through lifestyle changes and coping strategies, depression often requires professional intervention like therapy or medication to help improve symptoms and overall well-being. Mindfulness is a practice that can benefit anyone looking to improve their overall well-being and quality of life. It serves as a valuable tool for those looking to bring order and purpose into their lives.

This book provides valuable insights into managing stress by incorporating mindfulness into daily routines. However, readers are strongly encouraged to consult mental health professionals if they find themselves struggling with persistent feelings of overwhelm.

How Does This Book on Mindfulness Help in Dealing with Changes?

The author explores her journey of navigating the changes brought on by the pandemic and other challenging situations and how she utilised mindfulness practices to cope. She shares insights on how she centred her emotions by incorporating mindfulness techniques into her daily routine. At different points in time, she chose various tools to help her cope—finding solace in journalling to declutter her mind, seeking guidance from a counsellor to combat overwhelming negative thoughts, and turning to simple activities like walking to manage the challenges she faced.

Readers may resonate with the coping strategies when dealing with uncertainty, outlined in the subsequent chapters, and may consider incorporating them into their daily routines. This book may be suitable for individuals who want to understand the tools available to build resilience in the face of adversity and how these tools provide acceptance during times of transition.

What Time Commitment Do I Need to Embrace Mindfulness?

Embracing mindfulness, especially when you are already busy, can seem like a daunting task. However, it is important to remember that mindfulness does not have to be time-consuming or complicated. Incorporating small moments of mindfulness into your daily routine can help increase productivity and decrease stress levels. One way to embrace mindfulness when you are busy is to practise mindful breathing for a few minutes throughout the day. This straightforward exercise can help you refocus on the present moment and reduce feelings of being overwhelmed.

Additionally, setting aside time each day for a short meditation or yoga practice can also be beneficial in promoting mindfulness and reducing stress.

Remember, embracing mindfulness is not about adding more to your plate, rather it is about finding moments of stillness and presence within your busy schedule.

My Serendipitous Mindfulness Journey

'Peace comes from within. Do not seek it without.'
—Buddha

Mindfulness is not just a passing trend but a transformative lifestyle change. Nurturing a growth mindset enables individuals to evolve and adapt to the ever-changing demands of the world. From how we cook and eat to how we manage waste, choose products, seek experiences, and even burn calories—every aspect of our lives can be influenced by mindfulness.

Everyone has a story, and this is mine. I am sharing some personal accounts to make this mindfulness journey more relatable. This will hopefully serve as a guideline to those struggling to centre themselves. While I do not have all the answers, nor do I claim to have them, what I do know is that we are the only ones who can get ourselves out of this challenging phase. Our thoughts define our choices. Our choices define our actions. Our actions define our experiences. Our experiences define our journey on this earth. It's in our hands to make this journey a pleasant one.

I would like my readers to know that this mindfulness journey is not just a researched topic but also a personal journey that I have undertaken to be a better human. I started this mindfulness journey because I wanted to pass on an important legacy to my child—that of integrity, truth, persistence, resilience, and most importantly, being kind to oneself.

I was initially hesitant to share these personal stories as I would be exposing my vulnerabilities and revisiting all the difficult moments and questions of self-doubt. Author Brené Brown once wrote, 'Vulnerability is the birthplace of love, belonging, joy, courage, empathy, and creativity. It is the source of hope, empathy, accountability, and authenticity. If we want greater clarity in our purpose or deeper and more meaningful spiritual lives, vulnerability is the path.' Whilst validation from others is not necessary when the intention to expose your vulnerabilities serves a higher purpose, it is important to ensure that exposing these vulnerabilities does not come across as an appeal to pity.

Embarking on this journey of mindful living has been a profound experience. While I may not consider myself a mindfulness expert, I am committed to integrating mindfulness into every facet of my daily life. Whether it is making conscious choices in consumerism, prioritising environmental sustainability, practising healthy habits like sleep and nutrition, or fostering meaningful connections with others, mindfulness has become a guiding principle for me.

In her book, *The Light We Carry: Overcoming in Uncertain Times*, Michelle Obama eloquently expresses the gradual process of self-discovery and personal growth. She writes, 'I've progressed only slowly to where I am today. You will spend years gathering data about who you are and how you operate and only slowly will you find your way towards more certainty and a stronger sense of self. Only gradually will you begin to discover and use your light!' Her words resonate deeply with my journey towards mindfulness.

Through this serendipitous path, I have gained a deeper understanding of my emotions and desires, particularly during the challenges brought on by the pandemic. As I navigated through this period of uncertainty, I realised the importance of finding inner strength and embracing my true self. Since the support system I once relied on was no longer available, I embraced tapping into my own reservoir of resilience. This process of self-acceptance and self-belief has been pivotal in my journey towards mindfulness, allowing me to let go of the need for external validation. I now own my failures and wrongs as deeply as I celebrate my successes.

In essence, mindfulness is not just a practice; it is a reflective shift in perspective that empowers us to navigate life's complexities with grace and authenticity. Through mindfulness, we can illuminate our path, discover our true selves, and ultimately, carry our light with unwavering confidence.

The challenges that we have faced as a family, or that I have faced individually, have helped me to 'carry my light' further. When the strength I had relied on earlier from my birth family was no longer available, I had to find the inner strength within and use it to carry my light to accept who I am and what I want to be and believe in. The first step in that journey was nipping off the desire to seek validation.

When you embark on a journey of seeking and remaining true to your thoughts and intentions, if it is meant to be, the universe opens itself up and bestows abundance upon you. Recently, a dear friend—who has now become a mentor—approached me for assistance in writing content for her organisation's social media platforms, which focused on mindfulness. She is a respected thought leader in the field of education, advocating strongly for the integration of mindfulness practices in schools and higher education institutions. This collaboration served as a validation of my serendipitous journey towards mindfulness. Each day presents itself as an opportunity for learning and growth as I strive to enhance both myself and the world around me.

Mindfulness to my family is not merely a practice, but a lifestyle choice that requires breaking old patterns, making difficult decisions, and reinventing oneself. This process is far from easy, as it necessitates a series of daily changes aimed at freeing oneself from unnecessary thoughts and achieving emotional empowerment. My journey towards mindfulness began several years ago, unknowingly. While the challenges I face are deeply rooted, the solutions to them are often deceptively simple.

I consciously choose to focus on my victories rather than my setbacks, maintaining a positive outlook on my journey. There are some steps I have taken to embark on my mindfulness journey, which I continue to pursue as a lifelong learner. These are elaborated on in the next chapter.

Losing Myself

Over several years, a series of significant changes occurred in my life. The emotional toll of these changes began to affect my physical health, leading to the development of a severe hormonal imbalance, a common occurrence for women of my age. This imbalance, coupled with weight gain, exacerbated my physical issues. Despite my efforts to maintain a healthy lifestyle through chanting shlokas, diet, and exercise, I found myself struggling with countless health problems including weight gain, plantar fasciitis, hair loss, GERD, and asthma. My sleep patterns were disrupted, my eating habits were affected, and my anxiety levels soared, making it difficult to focus on my daily tasks.

Concerned individuals in my life suggested seeking professional help, a recommendation that initially puzzled me as I believed I was adequately managing my responsibilities. However, it became apparent that I was fixating on my problems and struggling to cope with the fallout from the pandemic and strained relationships within my birth family. This shift towards the individualistic behaviour of the family was unfamiliar and challenging for me to accept.

It became clear that I needed to address my mental health and seek support to navigate these difficult circumstances.

Finding Myself

A close friend, who is more like family to me, recommended counselling. Initially, I was hesitant and thought to myself, *Me? Counselling? I don't need it!* I had always been the person others turned to for advice, so I couldn't understand why I needed a counsellor. However, my friend explained that I needed someone who could listen without judgment, provide neutral perspectives on my decisions, and help me declutter my thoughts to be kinder to myself. That's when I realised the value of seeking professional help.

After living outside of India for over two and half decades, my friends had become my family. We had shared experiences in various countries, and they were the only constant in my life. This dear friend played a crucial role in guiding me on this transformative journey, and I am grateful for her support.

Mental health is complex, and everyone's struggles are unique. It is essential to recognise the impact of our internal narratives and seek help when we need it. Despite knowing I needed assistance, I struggled to overcome my reluctance to reach out to a professional. I kept revising the need to seek help, simply because the work at home and meting out my responsibilities were never affected. I failed to see that this stress was hurting my physical health. Temporary measures to alleviate physical issues, I soon realised, were not a sustainable solution to the issue. I needed to equip myself with tools to cope, that could help me through this unfathomable feeling. I felt lost and unsure of how to proceed.

Once I started getting the help I needed, I began a journey of self-discovery. I started paying closer attention to how I did things when I did them, and why I did them. This process allowed me to become more aware of my body, mind, and emotions. While it may have seemed like I had a clear plan for those observing me, I felt I was navigating this path without a clear roadmap.

What followed was a series of fortunate events that shaped my journey. While I didn't have a structured approach initially, each step I took led me closer to understanding myself better. This experience marked the beginning of my mindfulness journey, where I learnt to cultivate awareness and compassion towards myself.

Seeking Help

While growing up, we were expected to excel in all aspects of our academic and personal lives. The pressure to perform at a high level can lead us to believe that we must be perfect in everything we do. However, it is important to recognise that perfection is an unrealistic standard that can be detrimental to our mental health and overall well-being. I often tell my family that I like to perform a task up to a point where I don't need to repeat it. Now, what I've started consciously doing is, once I reach that point where the task is complete, how much effort I put into embellishing it is based on the time I reserve for it.

The first step towards mindfulness involves acknowledging our imperfections. When we sense a misalignment between our aspirations and actions, resulting in obstacles in our relationships with others and/or ourselves, it may be beneficial to seek assistance. Recognising our vulnerabilities and limitations can help us take proactive steps towards self-improvement, personal growth, and overall well-being.

Professionals possess the expertise and training necessary to offer impartial and unbiased guidance. Skilled counsellors and therapists can also identify any traits that may hinder our progress towards mindfulness, such as narcissism, low self-esteem, or behaviours indicative of intergenerational trauma.

I actively sought assistance from trained professionals to provide me with a valuable perspective on my thoughts and actions. This has become a crucial aspect of maintaining my mental well-being, as it challenges the ingrained thought patterns I developed during my formative years.

Finding the Wound

I believe I was going through an existential crisis. I had intense feelings of sadness and wanted to desperately be in control of things that I could not change. It is believed that an existential crisis is sometimes akin to an identity crisis, where the individual starts questioning the sense of values, beliefs, or even the self. As a priority, I embarked on a search for a counsellor to gain a deeper understanding of my thoughts. It was essential for me to find someone from my cultural background who could truly grasp the significance of phrases like, 'My comfort food is curd rice.' Each culture possesses intricate nuances that can only be fully comprehended through lived experiences. Fortunately, I came across a remarkable counsellor in India who specialised in Cognitive Behavioural Therapy (CBT). I promptly engaged her services online, feeling a sense of pride in taking this step towards self-improvement.

I specifically chose a counsellor who utilises CBT due to its effectiveness in addressing psychological issues. This technique operates on the fundamental principle that mental health challenges stem from prolonged patterns of negative thinking or maladaptive emotional behaviours. Extensive research also supports that individuals can overcome these challenges by developing coping strategies to counteract faulty thinking patterns and emotional responses.

The counsellor took me through an intensive program of Mindfulness-Based Cognitive Therapy (MBCT). This is a cutting-edge approach to psychotherapy that combines cognitive therapy techniques with mindfulness practices. With the help of the counsellor and this evidence-based technique, I learnt how to become more aware of my thoughts and feelings without judgment, break free from negative thought patterns, and develop healthier coping strategies. These techniques teach us to focus on the present moment by cultivating mindfulness skills. Learning this skill means we are firstly kinder to ourselves, better suited to respond to triggers in our lives, recognise a trigger when it presents itself, and take proactive measures to mitigate its effects.

Through multiple sessions with the counsellor, I not only shattered the stigma surrounding seeking professional help to declutter my mind from persistent negative thoughts but also unearthed aspects of myself that required attention. Despite the advancements in society, there remains a pervasive reluctance to acknowledge the need for counselling. Seeking help is often viewed as a sign of weakness or incompetence, perpetuating a sense of failure. I strongly encourage individuals who feel the need for support to seek out a reputable counsellor without shame. Seeking help is not a sign of weakness, but a strength that can lead to valuable learning experiences and foster connections with others.

Unravelling the Open Wound

During counselling, I discovered the process of unravelling and addressing areas in need of healing. This process of unravelling the built-up layers of wounds was both challenging and rewarding. I experienced a range of emotions while reflecting on past experiences and working through unresolved issues. This journey has required patience, self-awareness, and a willingness to confront difficult emotions head-on.

My counsellor has helped me identify patterns of behaviour, thought processes, and triggers that contribute to emotional distress, allowing me to uncover the root causes of my struggles. Through introspection, therapy sessions, and ongoing support, I have begun to heal from past trauma and negative experiences.

Throughout this process, my counsellor has emphasised the importance of being gentle with myself as I navigate the path towards healing and self-discovery.

This journey has been transformative, and I am grateful for the guidance and support that has helped me grow and heal. I continue to observe the triggers of my emotional state. As I age, I realise I have certain physical limitations that I must graciously accept and educate others around me about my capacity/boundaries. I have developed zero tolerance for negative conversations and now have the strength to not engage further—or engage very minimum level—with those who upset my mental balance. I have also observed that I enjoy my moments of silence and solitude a lot more than I ever did before. The loquaciousness of my nature has changed, and I embrace that completely. I have learnt to accept that my diet requires a lot more care than before and I do need to dedicate exclusive time for the same. I have observed very deeply that the flaws I have carried over from past generations need continuous work and effort to ensure my child is not ensnared in that, too.

I hold deep appreciation for the experiences that have moulded me thus far, and I eagerly anticipate embracing the opportunities that life has in store for me. Looking towards the future with optimism, I understand the significance of addressing and healing aspects of myself that stem from unresolved traumas passed down through generations.

Seeking guidance from a counsellor has been instrumental in helping me navigate my emotions and maintain a sense of stability in my mind. The validation I received from the counsellor reassured me that what I was feeling was not insignificant, which in turn fuelled my commitment to my mindfulness journey. I continue to seek guidance from a counsellor at key points in my life when I am struggling to cope with my emotions and experience a sense of overwhelm or when my family must make life-changing decisions—trust me, there are many. I do believe and advocate that seeking help from a counsellor, even when things are going well, is good practice, simply because it is easier for the counsellor to keep in touch with the client's life and can see how the client reacts when things are going well.

Knowing that the power to effect change lies within my own hands has empowered me to take control of my emotional well-being.

1

Change Is the Only Constant

'The changes we dread most may contain our salvation.'

—Barbara Kingsolver

In the words of the Greek Philosopher, Heraclitus, 'The only constant in life is change.' It is an inevitable and pervasive force in our lives. As we strive for personal and professional growth, we must embrace the idea that change is not to be feared, instead, it is to be embraced. We can adapt, learn, and thrive in an ever-changing society through change.

Life presents us with various challenges, and it is essential to discover the inner strength to overcome them, regain emotional balance, and move forward. Developing a mindset that is flexible, resilient, and open to new possibilities greatly allows the adaptability to change. By cultivating a growth mindset, individuals can embrace change as an opportunity for growth and development rather than a setback.

There have been moments when we have unknowingly practised mindfulness to find peace amidst chaos. This is a practice we have embraced and continue to uphold. It is important to acknowledge our emotions and seek guidance when needed to navigate life's obstacles with resilience and grace.

I have learnt to observe my thoughts and emotions without judgment, allowing me to respond to challenges with clarity and compassion. By incorporating mindfulness techniques such as meditation, deep breathing exercises, and mindful movement into my routine, I do believe I have experienced a deep shift in my mindset and perspective. This journey has not only transformed my personal life but has also strengthened my ability to manage stress, communicate more effectively with others, and make decisions from a place of alignment with my values and that of my family as a whole. It is through this ongoing commitment to mindfulness that I continue to grow and evolve both personally and professionally.

Despite the numerous challenges my family and I have encountered over the past two and a half decades, we have taken the time to appreciate the beauty around us, finding happiness in the smallest moments.

I encourage you to look for the positive aspects in every situation and urge you to see the silver lining to every cloud that has been shared.

Travelling Spouse

I have been a travelling spouse for nearly two decades, a decision my husband and I made deliberately. As an expatriate, the experience offers numerous advantages. One key benefit is the opportunity to immerse oneself in new cultures and environments with each move. This exposure broadens one's perspective and encourages expansive thinking.

Coming from a conservative background, being a travelling spouse has pushed me outside my comfort zone, enabling me to see the world through a different lens. I've discovered skills I never knew existed within me, and developed a diverse range of abilities from living abroad. Life as an expat has taught me or honed my adaptability, problem-solving skills, and effective communication across cultural boundaries, helping me navigate complex situations with confidence.

Managing various situations independently has nurtured a greater sense of self-reliance. Being far from home and familiar support systems continuously challenges me to rely on my resourcefulness, courage, and resilience, deepening my understanding of my capabilities.

We often let others' opinions sway us and may pass judgment without genuinely connecting with individuals. This tendency can be problematic when we've lived in the same community for an extended period. It is essential to recognise how external influences shape our perceptions and to approach each person with an open mind and genuine curiosity before forming opinions.

Relocating provides expats with the unique opportunity to reintroduce themselves to new societies as their authentic selves. People evolve, leaving behind emotional burdens from previous experiences. Embracing this evolved self allows us to forge meaningful connections in new environments. This process of reinvention is a valuable aspect of the expatriate experience, enabling us to navigate challenges abroad with confidence and resilience.

Being an expat has taught us to be more aware of external influences on our perceptions and to approach each individual with empathy and openness. By doing so, we cultivate richer relationships, free from quick judgments and preconceived notions.

Living abroad can be transformative, offering opportunities for personal and professional growth. However, it also comes with challenges that significantly impact various aspects of life. Our decision to relocate was driven by financial necessities and a desire for professional growth. We welcomed each challenge as an opportunity to advance our careers and maintain financial stability.

One major challenge was the constant uprooting and rebuilding of our lives. This included finding suitable schooling for our child, maintaining her education, and establishing new social connections. Additionally, relocating our homes and pets, and finding new healthcare providers for my family, while prioritising our well-being, added to the complexity.

In some cities, unfamiliarity with local culture and language made everyday tasks more difficult and hindered our sense of belonging. The strain of moving also impacted relationships back home, causing feelings of disconnect and communication difficulties, especially between our parents and our child.

My career and professional development were significantly affected. Although this was a conscious decision, the implications on my career growth were vastly underestimated. Constant reinvention and establishing my identity became more challenging.

Despite these trials, we have consistently risen to the occasion with grace and determination. Each relocation has presented its own set of obstacles, but we have approached them with resilience and a positive attitude, emerging stronger and more adaptable with each move.

Some mindfulness techniques my family and I embrace daily include expressing gratitude for our experiences and opportunities. When asked which city we've lived in is the best, we always say that each country has its positives and negatives, but wherever we are currently living is the best place we've ever experienced. We strive to live in the 'now' and fully embrace each location, creating a sense of 'home' wherever we go. We acknowledge and accept the emotions that accompany leaving a familiar home and starting fresh without judgment.

As someone deeply connected to my Indian roots, I've faced the challenge of relocating frequently while staying true to my values. My culture and traditions run deep, and I've made a conscious effort to reflect our beliefs in every home while embracing new cultures. For instance, while wine with dinner was uncommon in India, living in France allowed us to appreciate wine-making. We educated ourselves on wine pairings for Indian cuisine when hosting guests. Despite not consuming alcohol myself, I humorously say I am 'intoxicated' by my love for my family and the world around me. Adapting to different cultures while maintaining one's values is essential for preserving authenticity and ensuring seamless integration into new environments.

Transitioning between locations has required meticulous scrutiny of every detail, reassessing finances, reviewing paperwork, and evaluating belongings repeatedly. Each move necessitated careful decluttering to avoid transporting unnecessary items, helping us stay within budget and streamline our process. Maintaining routines has been crucial for stability and adaptation. We've learnt to simplify our lives and carry only what is truly necessary.

Ralph Waldo Emerson once said, 'He who is not every day conquering some fear has not learnt the secret of life.' I can say with certainty that we are on the path to understanding the secret of life.

Blindsided

In 2001, my husband and I immigrated to Canada with our young child. At the time, we depended heavily on my husband's job as our primary income source, with only modest savings in the bank.

The evening my husband called me, on the Ides of March remains vivid. He urgently needed medical attention, which led to a diagnosis of retinal detachment. Thankfully, the exceptional medical care in Canada ensured he received timely treatment.

During his recovery at home, his boss unexpectedly visited us. While we were taken aback by her presence, we extended our hospitality and respect, as we had been taught in India. During this visit, we learnt that the company was shutting down.

This unforeseen event left us uncertain about our future. We assessed our financial situation, determining how long we could sustain ourselves with our current resources. To cut costs, we downsized to a smaller rented apartment and managed our finances diligently while prioritising our relationship and shielding our child from our challenges.

Despite the hardships, we remained resilient and focused on building a stable future. Our journey in Canada had its ups and downs, but through perseverance and determination, we overcame obstacles and grew stronger as a family.

During this chaotic period, we made a conscious effort to prioritise our relationships. We engaged in activities that weren't expensive but at the same time brought happiness. Despite our limited resources, we found joy in these simple pleasures that brought us closer.

Relying on our commitment to each other, we navigated each challenge. We meticulously planned doctor's visits, prepared questions, and sought additional information from medical professionals. We even considered learning braille, though (thankfully) it proved unnecessary.

An obstacle that once seemed insurmountable remains a significant memory, but we have successfully overcome it. My husband continues to attend regular check-ups and remains vigilant about his health. As expats, we ensure that we research and identify retinal specialists in each new city we relocate to, ensuring uninterrupted follow-up care. We continue to embrace resilience and take necessary steps to ensure our well-being.

Understanding that retinal issues can be present from birth, we scheduled regular check-ups for our daughter starting at age two. When she was about ten, she mentioned seeing a dark cloud in her eyes. We arranged an emergency eye appointment at a leading hospital in Dubai, where doctors discovered retinal tears that required urgent treatment. Despite the initial shock, we received the necessary guidance to address the issue.

During my daughter's recovery, my family struggled with the sudden diagnosis. It was during this time that I found solace in writing my second book, *The Rose Petal Trails—A Sutra for Timeless Love*. Inspired by the Kama Sutra, this poetic fiction became a creative outlet for me. With determination and the support of my husband, who edited my work, I completed the book in just 14 days.

Writing the book not only distracted me from our daughter's recovery but also brought me and my husband closer as we collaborated on the project. Reflecting on that period, I find that the memories of working on the book stand out more vividly than those of our daughter's health struggles. It was a time of healing and growth for our family, highlighting the strength found in creativity and collaboration during challenging times.

Surgical Menopause

After my daughter left for university to pursue her undergraduate studies, I envisioned a newfound sense of freedom and opportunity. However, life had other plans in store. Following over a year-long battle with menstrual issues, my gynaecologist recommended that I undergo a hysterectomy. She assured me that I had earned this procedure, as I had endured a lot of pain.

The surgery involved a total hysterectomy, during which both the uterus and cervix were removed. The excruciating pain I had been enduring was attributed to severe adenomyosis and endometriosis, which even heavy medication could not alleviate.

While the hysterectomy provided much-needed relief, the road to recovery was challenging. We had relocated to a new country, leaving us without a support system. Thankfully, my friends proved to be unwavering pillars of support, and our neighbours also lent a helping hand. Unfortunately, my birth family was absent both emotionally and physically during this difficult time, and issues with them were only exacerbated following the surgery.

Navigating through a whirlwind of emotions, ranging from physical discomfort to feelings of isolation, became my new reality. After the surgery, I struggled to take even a few steps. I vividly remember relying on a smartwatch with a step counter to monitor my progress.

I did not hesitate to seek help online and joined an online support group called 'Hyster Sisters', which proved invaluable. I sought guidance on many aspects of recovery from the operation that I couldn't ask anyone else—from managing pain medication to coping with rashes resulting from fluctuating estrogenic levels. I did not feel alone. I realised several people have gone through similar situations, which helped me cope better.

Despite trying various remedies, such as using copious amounts of coconut oil to soothe my skin, I found myself grappling with the persistent rashes. A costly cream was recommended to address this issue, presenting a financial challenge. This was a pivotal moment in my journey towards recovery and self-care.

During my research, I discovered the potential of creating my own moisturising cream. I began by crafting shea butter-based organic creams and gradually delved into the process of creating other cosmetic products that I incorporate into my daily routine. This marked the beginning of my journey into the world of cosmetic formulation.

Before my surgery, I had been practising yoga for several years. However, I felt the need to take my practice to the next level. That's when I was introduced to my current yoga teacher Raksha Agarwal. Her teachings played a crucial role in my speedy recovery post-surgery.

Under Raksha's guidance, I learnt various yoga techniques that helped alleviate my pain and discomfort. She also introduced me to meditation practices such as savasana, akin to body scan meditation, enhancing my mind-body awareness.

Leveraging my background in nutrition, I made dietary changes to incorporate anti-inflammatory foods. Additionally, I utilised mindfulness and diet apps to track my progress and set achievable goals for continuous improvement.

Two months after my surgery, I was fully immersed in preparing for an international move, yet again.

Thanks to mindfulness practices, I was able to shift my focus from the surgery and having become empty nesters, to the upcoming relocation to France, allowing me to tackle this new challenge with vigour and determination.

The 'C' word

While staying at a hotel in France during our relocation, I received a distressing call from my niece in India. She informed me that my mother, who was being treated by my niece's husband for eye issues, had been diagnosed with cancer in her eye and required intensive chemotherapy sessions. Unfortunately, due to visa complications, I couldn't leave France to be with my family during this difficult time. As an expat, I am familiar with the challenges of feeling disconnected from my family back home—despite the physical distance, the emotional toll of being unable to support our loved ones during times of need is a burden we carry.

After many tears, I realised that the best course of action was to focus on the tasks at hand. Ensuring a smooth transition into France, which involved finding a home and settling in, became my top priority. I understood that dwelling on my feelings of despair would not change the situation, so I channelled my energy into achieving my current goals. It was challenging to remain focused amidst the emotional turmoil, but I persevered to ensure my family adjusted well to our new environment. Despite the challenges, I found solace in knowing I was doing everything to provide stability and support during uncertainty.

The Pandemic

On 11 March 2020, while waiting at the railway station to pick up my husband, I heard the World Health Organisation (WHO) declare COVID-19 a pandemic. Though I didn't fully grasp the gravity of the situation, I distinctly remember a growing sense of fear and anxiety. This was at a time when my nerves were already frayed with all the changes that we were already going through.

Caring for ageing in-laws and parents, alongside supporting our child, weighed heavily on me. Seeking solace in routine activities and volunteering, I tried to find a sense of normality amidst the chaos. Balancing these roles became daunting, leading to a cycle of exhaustion.

The challenges continued as my in-laws struggled to live independently and needed to be relocated to another city in India. Coordinating this move remotely was complex, as their physical, emotional, and mental well-being required constant attention. Despite our resourcefulness in managing the move seamlessly, the toll on my own health was undeniable.

Tragedy struck when my father and a beloved aunt, who had been a mentor to me, succumbed to COVID-19. The inability to bid them a proper farewell or provide support to my in-laws during their relocation added to the weight of the situation. The pandemic has left an indelible mark on each of us, far exceeding any expectations of its impact.

During these challenging times, my family and I, like many others, faced multiple layers of distress. Yet we consciously expressed gratitude for our blessings, recognising that others were facing even greater hardships. By focusing on gratitude, we prevented ourselves from succumbing to despair.

Our top priority became our physical and emotional health. We understood the importance of time management in adapting to the new dynamics within our family and the increased responsibilities we faced. Self-care activities such as exercise, meditation, and tending to our plants and pets became essential in combating burnout and isolation. We found that caring for our pets and plants not only brought us joy but also served as effective stress relievers, leading us to explore composting as a new hobby.

To ensure our well-being, we meticulously planned and managed our daily routines. This involved creating clear schedules, prioritising tasks, and setting boundaries to maintain balance. With the entire family working from home, we had to adjust to the demands of remote work while striving to maintain a sense of normality, control, and resilience during the pandemic.

My niece, who is actively engaged in nature walks and practices forest bathing professionally through her company, Nature Connections, has spoken highly of how this practice has helped her heal in numerous ways. During the pandemic, we took advantage of the nearby forests to partake in this rejuvenating experience. As the term suggests, forest bathing involves immersing oneself in the healing effects of nature within the forest. The benefits are plentiful, and we returned from our walks feeling refreshed and invigorated. We recognise that this is a luxury not everyone has access to, and we are deeply grateful for the enriching experiences we have enjoyed.

Loss of Furry Friends

When our daughter was just six years old, we moved to the Far East. As she was very fond of pets, my husband and I decided to get her a dog to help her adjust to the big change of leaving her friends and the place she grew up in. We promised her a dog once we had settled into our new home.

After we moved, we began searching for a dog to adopt and found an adorable poodle-terrier mix puppy. He was one of a litter of twelve, and we fell in love with him instantly. We named him Mocha and shared fourteen wonderful years with him, making unforgettable memories. Later, when we moved to another country after our home was broken into, we decided to get a German Shepherd. Java was a lively and lovable dog who brought joy and chaos into our lives.

Our days were filled with both challenging and happy moments with our furry companions. They became like siblings to our daughter, filling our home with love and laughter. In a world that can feel overwhelming, our dogs provided a sense of calm and helped us stay present in the moment. They truly helped us reconnect with ourselves and the world around us. Through their daily actions and behaviours, they exemplified mindfulness, serving as a constant reminder to remain present and engaged.

Each morning, they warmly greeted us with a hug, a rollover on the floor, and sometimes a bark to signal the need for a walk. Their enthusiasm upon our return home was palpable as if they could communicate their joy and how much they missed us during our brief absence. They savoured every bite of their food and approached all activities with acceptance and eagerness. Whether playing hide and seek or fetch, or simply sitting quietly together, their playful and serene demeanour brought us joy and relaxation. They taught us to embrace each moment wholeheartedly.

Despite their endearing qualities, the dogs had distinct personalities that occasionally clashed. Their alpha male tendencies required us to maintain separate living arrangements for the dogs to prevent conflicts. Funnily, we referred to our home as a 'gated community', as we strategically placed child gates to ensure their separation from each other.

Reflecting on these experiences now, we can appreciate the humour in the situation. However, for nine years, we diligently navigated the delicate balance of keeping the dogs apart. Through it all, they taught us valuable lessons in patience, acceptance, and the importance of setting boundaries when necessary.

Three months after my father's passing in 2021, on a scorching summer day, our beloved Mocha suffered a stroke and passed away suddenly. Mocha had been a cherished member of our family for fourteen wonderful years, and we had created countless beautiful memories together. After Mocha's passing, Java remained with us for a brief period, providing comfort and companionship as we grieved. However, six months later, Java began experiencing muscular issues and other unidentified health problems that proved untreatable. Sadly, Java succumbed to his illness the following summer.

Dogs teach us many lessons in mindfulness: to love unconditionally, to accept situations without judgment, and most importantly, to seize the day.

The loss of a pet can be an incredibly heart-wrenching experience. Dogs hold a special place in our hearts, offering companionship, unconditional love, and boundless joy. Their absence leaves a profound void in our lives, affecting our daily routines and emotional well-being. While some may underestimate the depth of grief felt over the loss of a pet, those who have experienced it understand the profound emotional impact it can have.

In our busy lives, it can be easy to overlook the need to properly grieve the loss of a beloved pet. However, it is essential to acknowledge and process the emotions that come with such a loss. Mourning the passing of a pet is a valid and important part of the healing process, allowing us to honour the bond we shared with our furry companions. It is crucial to give ourselves the time and space to grieve.

The Love Story

The caste system in India, a longstanding social hierarchy rooted in ancient Hindu society, has historically divided individuals into distinct groups based on birth and occupation, limiting mobility between castes. Although laws were enacted in 1948 to prohibit caste-based discrimination, and the Indian constitution solidified this in 1950, the caste system still significantly influences social interactions, marriage preferences, economic prospects, and political representation. Despite ongoing efforts to promote equality through affirmative action and educational initiatives, instances of honour killings persist in some areas of India.

Six decades ago, inter-caste marriages posed significant challenges for my parents. The rigid caste system enforced strict norms, making it unacceptable for my parents, who belonged to different castes, to marry and sustain their union.

Despite these challenges, my parents courageously defied societal expectations and norms by pursuing love across caste boundaries. They fought tirelessly for acceptance and inclusion, overcoming every obstacle with determination and grace. Their journey serves as a testament to their strength, resilience, and unwavering commitment to each other.

The union of two souls brought its own set of challenges for both them and us, their offsprings. My parents faced ostracism and marginalisation due to their inter-caste marriage, which deeply affected their well-being and self-esteem, impacting me as well. However, I am grateful for the diverse perspective this upbringing afforded me. Growing up in a multicultural environment has shaped my approach to personal and professional endeavours. It has allowed me to appreciate different customs, traditions, and ideologies, promoting open-mindedness and adaptability. This background has provided unique insights into human behaviour and communication, enabling me to engage effectively with individuals from varying backgrounds.

Social hierarchies play a significant role in shaping various aspects of any marriage, especially in an inter-caste one. Power dynamics, decision-making processes, and societal perceptions all influence our identities. I have grappled with complex issues related to racial identity, societal acceptance, language, culinary preferences, friendships, and the stark disparities between my parents' extended families.

The cultural differences between my parents' families hindered what would be considered normal communication. Lack of cultural cohesion and a constant need to be on guard as to which side of the family (caste) I was supporting, created a sense of disconnect and alienation within the family dynamics. Casteism especially weighed heavily on my growing years as I felt judged no matter what I did, on both sides of the families of my parents.

As the saying goes, it is all a package deal. While I learnt to appreciate different cultures and navigate the complexities of social hierarchies established by inter-caste marriages, this gestalt experience has significantly influenced who I have become today, shaping my identity and perspective.

Recognising Generational Trauma

Generational trauma refers to the passing down of traumatic experiences and their effects from one generation to the next. The emotional impact of my parents' inter-caste marriage was intense, affecting not just them but also me as their offspring. Through multiple counselling sessions, I have come to realise that I carry the weight of generational trauma, that must be dealt with sensitively.

My coping mechanisms, learnt behaviours, and reactions to various stimuli mirrored those of my ancestors, which no longer align with today's societal norms or with the behavioural patterns inherited by my husband. This disparity in our approaches to handling complex and stressful situations has led to heightened stress and anxiety in the past.

Acknowledging and addressing generational trauma is imperative to breaking the cycle and fostering healing within families. Self-awareness, a fundamental aspect of mindfulness, has enabled me to recognise the behavioural patterns I needed to change to prevent them from being passed on to future generations. This awareness, coupled with timely action, can lead to improved mental health outcomes for future generations.

Family in Distress

The breakdown of familial relationships due to long-standing generational trauma and stress, exacerbated by factors such as financial challenges, relocation from our homeland, and the multifarious challenges that come with caring for ageing parents, has led to a significant divide within my birth family. This discord has fostered a sense of estrangement, leaving me with unanswered questions and disbelief at the disintegration of our once close-knit family unit.

As family dynamics have shifted over time, misunderstandings, conflicts, and unresolved issues have deepened the chasm between my family members and me. The ongoing turmoil has not only impacted my personal growth and development but has also strained even the simplest interactions with my extended family. The mindless banter that once warmed our hearts is now a thing of the past.

These are challenges, whether big or small is relative. They need to be overcome, and I realised that the only way to do so is by working on myself. I'm thankful for my learnings in Hindu philosophy that constantly remind us about detachment. I am grateful not only for the opportunities and challenges that have come my way but also for allowing me to focus on the things that matter and not succumb to the effect of karma in others' lives.

2
Heal Your Mind, Mindfully

'The present moment is filled with joy and happiness. If you are attentive, you will see it.'

—Thích Nhất Hạnh

Through my experiences as an expatriate, I have learnt the importance of adapting regardless of the circumstances. We endeavoured to see the silver lining to every cloud that hung over our heads.

Resetting Expectations

Our priorities and needs evolve as we journey through life, making it essential to realign our expectations accordingly. While this process of resetting expectations may be challenging, it is crucial to minimise disappointments and foster personal growth and fulfilment.

In today's fast-paced society, we are often inundated with societal norms and expectations, which can create immense pressure and stress. For instance, when my career goals shifted due to changing priorities, I needed to adjust my expectations regarding professional achievements to avoid feelings of inadequacy or failure. It was during this period of transition that I unexpectedly embarked on a new path as an author, a stark departure from my background in nutrition.

I often humorously remark that we must allow the universe time to change its course as our desires and circumstances may shift unexpectedly. I strongly believe—some may say it is a fatalistic approach—that we always get what we deserve, which may not necessarily be what we desire. The belief that there is a force protecting our every action has always helped me relinquish my control over a problem that is not humanly solvable.

The key to manifestation lies in our intense yearning for a particular outcome, which subconsciously propels us towards success. Embracing change and adapting our expectations to meet current needs empowers us to navigate life's uncertainties with poise and confidence, ultimately leading to the elusive pursuit of happiness and success.

Make Mindfulness Part of Your Daily Life

Consistently and consciously practising mindfulness is essential for maintaining overall well-being and mental clarity. We can fully reap the benefits of mindfulness through consistent practice as it requires ongoing effort and dedication to develop this skill. However, maintaining consistency can be challenging when faced with new obstacles.

Just as we may never forget to brush our teeth or perform other tasks that have become habits over the years, embracing mindfulness also requires time and effort to become a daily habit. According to the 21/90 rule in Psychology, it takes 21 days to form a habit and 90 days to make it a permanent lifestyle change. However, this rule assumes that the 100 days pass without any new challenges arising. The key to making lasting lifestyle changes is to take small steps and not attempt to make all changes at once.

By gradually incorporating mindfulness into our daily routine, we can cultivate a more mindful and balanced life. Consistency is key in developing a mindful way of being, as it helps to reinforce new habits and neural pathways in the brain. By incorporating mindfulness practices into daily routines, individuals can gradually train their minds to be more focused, aware, and compassionate.

Conscious mindfulness involves intentionally bringing awareness to one's thoughts, emotions, and sensations throughout the day. This conscious effort to practise mindfulness allows individuals to respond to challenges with greater clarity and insight, rather than reacting impulsively out of habit or fear. Being mindful in daily activities such as eating, walking, and interacting with others can enhance the quality of these experiences and deepen one's connection to the present moment. Conscious mindfulness helps us to respond to a situation rather than react to it.

Choosing a Practice Suitable to You

Individuality is key when it comes to embarking on the journey of mindfulness. It is essential to understand that one size does not fit all. Simply following in the footsteps of a friend may not necessarily lead to the same results for you. The decision to pursue mindfulness must stem from a deep internal desire, as true change can only come from within.

Each of us possesses unique learning preferences, strengths, and weaknesses that must be taken into account to facilitate effective learning. It is essential to assess our skills and abilities to ensure that the chosen practice aligns with our capabilities. It is important to recognise that everyone has their own pace of learning and level of adaptability, influenced by various factors such as family circumstances and personal situations.

The ideas presented in this book reflect what has been successful for me and my family based on our circumstances at the time. One way to personalise your mindfulness practice is to experiment with different techniques and discover what resonates best with you. By trying out various methods and paying attention to how they make you feel, you can identify practices that align most with your needs and incorporate them into your daily routine.

3
What Is Mindfulness?

'We use mindfulness to observe the way we cling to pleasant experiences & push away unpleasant ones.'

—Sharon Salzberg

Several books and websites define and demystify this often-searched word, mindfulness. Excess information can confuse us as we do not know where to start. Just like a particular diet or exercise regime does not work for everyone, similarly, mindfulness practice is also individual-based. The methods that I have adapted and used to embrace mindfulness may not work for everyone, but once we understand the premise of mindfulness and what it is not, we will be in a better position to embrace this journey.

Definition of Mindfulness

To begin with, let us understand the basic definition of mindfulness from the father of mindfulness himself, Thích Nhất Hạnh (Thay, as called by his students), a peace activist and Buddhist monk. He said, 'Mindfulness is the capacity to be aware of what is going on and what is there. The object of mindfulness can be anything.'

There are several definitions of mindfulness, but the one that stands out is mentioned in the first verse of Patanjali's

Yoga Sutra, which says, '*Atha yoga anushasanam*.' It translates to, 'Now, begins the instruction of yoga.' Many translations of this verse have been elaborated in different Sanskrit texts, but the key takeaway is to focus on the word 'now'. Be in the now. Take in every emotion, feeling, and awareness that comes to you. Acknowledge it, welcome it, and let it go. Just be aware not to attach any emotion to that thought. The emotion is what lingers on, not the actual thought.

I have noticed that while cooking I am completely absorbed in the task at hand to the point where I am easily startled by any unexpected interruptions. Psychologists may have various explanations for this reaction, but cooking is a therapeutic experience. This intense focus is a skill that I have honed over time, stemming from a fear of making irreversible mistakes instilled by the pressure of meeting generational expectations of perfection. Although the skill comes from a place of fear, I now acknowledge the advantage of conscious and diligent effort on any chosen task.

I learnt to fully appreciate the ingredients and flavours that I used. Presentation, too, plays a key role in all the dinners I host—focusing on the colours, textures, and aromas of the ingredients, I began to understand how they contribute to the overall taste and look of the dish. This nuanced understanding of the cooking process allowed me the liberty to experiment with fusion cooking, a process I have begun to enjoy a lot.

As I dedicated myself to each task with diligence, expertise followed naturally, and passion held hands with expertise to make the transition smoother. With expertise came increased self-confidence, leading to a boost in self-worth.

This newfound sense of self-worth has made me a happier individual, radiating positive energy that is reciprocated by those in my presence. It has created a virtuous cycle of positivity in my life. Cooking has become more than just a hobby; it has become a source of personal growth and fulfilment. It has helped me understand myself by being in the now.

Foundations of Mindfulness

In the Buddhist tradition, the four foundations of mindfulness are considered essential practices for developing mindfulness and awareness. These foundations serve as a roadmap for practitioners to cultivate a greater sense of presence and understanding in their daily lives.

According to Bhante Henepola Gunaratana, a Sri Lankan Theravada Buddhist monk, the four foundations of mindfulness are:

Mindfulness of the Body

Mindfulness of the body involves observing and understanding the signals our bodies send us closely. By tuning into these signs, individuals can gain a deeper insight into their physical sensations and reactions, ultimately leading to better stress and emotion management.

When we practise mindfulness of our bodies, we learn to pause and ask ourselves questions rather than simply reacting to our body's impulses. For instance, thirst can often be mistaken for hunger. Dehydration may manifest as low energy levels, prompting a strong urge to eat. By questioning ourselves, 'Am I truly hungry or just thirsty?' we can avoid unnecessary snacking and address our body's true needs.

Mindfulness of Feelings

Mindfulness of our feelings is a crucial component of emotional intelligence and self-awareness. By being mindful of our emotions, we can better understand and manage them, leading to healthier and more constructive responses. This practice involves observing our emotional experiences without judgment and accepting them without suppression or avoidance.

Renowned author Emily Maroutian once said, 'Allow yourself to feel what you feel instead of getting mad at yourself for not feeling what you should feel. Think your thoughts instead of worrying about what you should be thinking. Claim your decisions, choices, desires, thoughts, and feelings. You are not yours until you allow all that you are right here, right now.'

By cultivating mindfulness of our feelings, we can gain a deeper insight into ourselves and our emotional triggers, ultimately enhancing our emotional regulation and resilience. Meaningful relationships with others stem from a better understanding of ourselves. Recognising our emotional triggers and understanding our feelings allow us to empathise and connect with others on a deeper level, fostering authentic interactions, which help us identify truly beneficial relationships.

Implementing these solutions can be challenging, but self-care is an essential component in this process. It is important to set clear boundaries to protect our emotions and present our best selves to the world. By being mindful of our feelings, we can create a more harmonious and emotionally intelligent environment within ourselves and in our relationships.

There is a delicate balance between practising self-care and being selfish. It is important to ask ourselves certain questions to ensure that we navigate this path of self-care effectively. I continue to reflect on some of the questions mentioned below, and more in my journey of embracing mindfulness. It is important to prioritise our well-being while also being mindful of the impact our actions may have on others:

- Do I recognise that my current emotions, whether positive or negative, are temporary and will eventually pass?
- Am I equipped to assess a situation to determine if there is a viable solution, or can I let go if necessary? Additionally, am I able to accept that I cannot control every outcome and must relinquish some control to the universe after giving my best effort?

Mindfulness of the Mind

Mindfulness of the mind is a practice that involves being aware of one's thoughts, emotions, and mental processes in a non-judgmental way. It requires a willingness to observe the mind's activities without becoming entangled in them or reacting impulsively. By cultivating mindfulness of the mind, individuals can gain a deeper understanding of their thought patterns, reactions, and the impact of their mental states on overall well-being. This practice is particularly valuable during times of high stress and pressure. By practising mindfulness of the mind, we can enhance our ability to manage stress, maintain focus, and make well-informed decisions.

My journey into this aspect of mindfulness began with journalling my thoughts. I named my first journal '*Vichaaran*', which translates to 'contemplation'. I recorded my thoughts to improve mental clarity and declutter my mind. As I continued to write, I gained insight into areas where I needed assistance and where I needed to adjust. This led to the creation of my first book, *Shells on the Beach*, which consisted of poems and articles reflecting my journey of understanding my thoughts. This book not only helped me comprehend my thoughts better but also facilitated communication between my young daughter and my frequently travelling husband.

By practising mindfulness of the mind and reflecting on questions that they ask themselves, individuals can enhance their self-awareness, emotional intelligence, and overall well-being:

a. How do I effectively manage multiple tasks that require my attention simultaneously? Can I prioritise and focus on one task at a time, or do I feel compelled to address everything simultaneously?
b. When faced with challenging situations in relationships, do I react on an impulse or do I respond thoughtfully and calmly?
c. In times of personal turmoil at home, how do I handle my emotions? Do I concentrate on addressing the issue at hand, or do I find myself feeling scattered and overwhelmed?
d. When making decisions, do I rely on judgment and assumptions, or do I base my actions on evidence and facts?

Mindfulness of Dharma

Mindfulness of dharma involves recognising the interconnectedness of all beings and developing compassion and loving-kindness towards others. Through this practice, individuals can cultivate a sense of empathy and understanding, leading to a more harmonious and fulfilling life.

When faced with a metaphorical fork in the road, we are often tasked with making difficult decisions that can greatly impact our lives. These situations require critical thinking and a clear understanding of one's values and priorities. Whilst it is important to take the time to assess all potential outcomes and implications of each path before making a decision, sometimes it is not possible to predict the outcome of a decision till it is made. Decisions are often made with a leap of faith—and I don't just mean religious faith. Intuition and gut instincts when navigating these challenging situations also play a huge role in making decisions. However, decisions are not always consistent with our individual values and personal goals. Decisions are sometimes based on the cumulative values and goals of those in our inner circle.

The choices we make based on the decisions have consequences that we must be prepared to handle. That is when it becomes imperative to ask ourselves questions that ensure all those concerned—including ourselves—are following the path of truth.

When faced with challenging situations involving family or friends, I always ask the following questions:

a. Am I choosing the path that aligns with my values and beliefs?
b. Are my emotions, thoughts, and actions in harmony with my true self?
c. Do I feel empowered and at peace after addressing the issue, or has it left a negative impact?
d. Am I handling difficult situations with integrity and mindfulness, ensuring that my actions align with my moral compass?

The answers to these questions might tick the right boxes but could also strain relationships—as it did in my case—because they may not align with others' values. It is important to be aware during these times that the interdependency—or lack of it—in relationships can lead us to choose paths that may not be suitable for everyone, and that's okay, too, as long as we steer ourselves within the path of what is right.

4

10 Essential Self-Checks for a Successful Mindfulness Journey

'If you can't measure it, you can't manage it.'

—Peter Drucker

Measurement is key to understanding progress. Without measuring, how can one truly know how they are doing? I have specific criteria—physical, emotional, and mental—that determine if I am on the right path. These simple signs are signals from my body, mind, and emotions that guide me in adjusting my actions as I navigate life's challenges, both individually and as a family.

While these personal checks are tailored to my journey, they may also prove beneficial to others. Some of these indicators are quantifiable, while others are more subjective. However, the quantifiable measures often have a ripple effect on the non-quantifiable ones, meaning that correcting one aspect can lead to improvement in other areas.

Utilising tools such as fitness trackers to monitor daily steps, calories burned, resting heart rate, and cardio activity can provide valuable insights into one's physical well-being. Additionally, apps that track food intake and water consumption can help manage calorie intake and overall nutrition. The quality, quantity, and timing of food consumption all contribute to both physical and mental health.

It is important to remember that these tools and numerical data, including weight measurements, are simply aids in personal growth. The goal is to feel comfortable in one's own skin, rather than striving for external validation or extreme physical feats.

With this mindset, I continue my journey of personal growth by observing and tracking signs and symptoms that reflect my progress towards my goals.

Given below is a basic checklist that I use to ensure that physical and mental health are in sync, and if not, understand what measures I would need to take. The checklist provided here is explored in depth in the following chapters.

Blood Work

Regular health check-ups are an essential component of maintaining overall well-being and preventing potential health issues. By scheduling routine check-ups we can monitor our health status and detect any early signs of diseases or conditions. These health checks often include measurements of vital health indicators such as blood pressure, cholesterol levels, and body mass index, which can provide valuable information about an individual's current health status and potential risk factors for developing chronic illnesses. Sometimes, these are just the tip of the iceberg of a larger underlying issue.

These health check-ups also provide a better understanding of our physical state and help us take necessary preventative actions and make healthy lifestyle choices. By being proactive about scheduling routine check-ups with healthcare providers, we can take control of our health and work towards achieving optimal well-being. Physical health can greatly impact the mental state. Research has shown that reduced levels of vitamin D levels have a significant impact on not only thyroid and insulin production but also greatly affect mental health.

Although my blood work did not reveal any chemical imbalances, I found myself struggling to understand the reasons behind my weight gain and the associated health problems, such as plantar fasciitis, gastroesophageal reflux disease (GERD), and various other unwanted issues. I knew I needed to tackle each problem individually to address these challenges.

I began by addressing my digestive issues. Through a combination of intermittent fasting and reducing sugar intake, I was able to gain better control over my GERD and digestive problems. As the weight started to come off, I noticed a gradual improvement in my plantar fasciitis symptoms. Additionally, I invested in sandals with arch support that I could wear both at home and outdoors. It took several months of dedication and effort, but eventually, I found myself free from the pain of plantar fasciitis. This experience taught me the importance of taking a holistic approach to health and addressing issues one step at a time,

This is an ongoing journey and with age new challenges arise. We must meet those challenges by consistently giving importance to physical health. Strength training, yoga, and walking, along with a proper diet, help in maintaining optimal health as we age.

Sleep Health

Sleep is a fundamental aspect of human health, with numerous studies demonstrating its positive impact on overall well-being. One of the most important benefits of sleep is its role in cognitive function. During sleep, the brain consolidates memories and processes information, allowing individuals to better retain and recall information.

Sleep plays a significant role in emotional regulation and mental health and can help regulate mood and promote emotional stability. This is because sleep helps to balance the production of neurotransmitters essential for emotional well-being, such as serotonin and dopamine. By ensuring proper sleep hygiene, individuals can reduce the risk of developing mental health disorders and maintain a positive outlook on life.

Studies have shown that inadequate sleep can increase the risk of developing chronic conditions such as heart disease, diabetes, and obesity. This is because, during sleep, the body repairs itself, regulates hormone levels, and strengthens the immune system. By getting enough rest each night, individuals can improve their physical health, reduce inflammation in the body, and lower the risk of developing chronic diseases.

One of the best ways to determine if one has had a good sleep is to be aware of how you feel when you wake up every morning and if you can easily accomplish the tasks for the day. If you struggle to stay awake during the day or feel unusually hungry with increased sweet cravings, it is a sign that your body's required sleep levels were not met the previous night.

When my sleep was affected, I used the guided meditation app to help channel my thoughts better. This, along with breath work, helped me fall into the arms of sleep quickly.

Bowel Health

Having well-emptied bowels is essential for overall good health and well-being. When the bowels are not functioning properly, toxins can build up in the body that can further lead to a variety of health issues like bloating, gas, constipation, and serious conditions like irritable bowel syndrome or colorectal cancer. Ensuring that the bowels are emptied well regularly through a healthy diet, regular exercise, and proper hydration is essential for maintaining optimal digestive health and preventing these negative consequences.

There are several ways to promote healthy bowel movements, including consuming a diet high in fibre, staying hydrated, and getting regular exercise. Fibre promotes regular bowel movements by adding bulk to the stool, making it easier to pass through the digestive system. Drinking plenty of water keeps the stool soft and easy to pass, while exercise helps stimulate the digestive tract muscles, promoting regular bowel movements. By incorporating these habits into our daily routine, we can help ensure that our bowels are emptied well and promote overall digestive health and well-being.

Having an early dinner or embracing the circadian rhythm of intermittent fasting greatly helped my bowel movement. Additionally, I was more disciplined with the amount of water and sugar I consumed, thus effectively clearing the bowels. Paying attention to the colour and consistency of the excretion is as important as the frequency with which the bowels are relieved. Being aware of this is also as important as it could indicate symptoms of a bigger problem.

Nutritional Health

The amount of food and water the body needs daily depends on factors such as age, gender, weight, physical activity level, and overall health. Generally, an average adult needs around 2,000–2,500 calories daily to maintain their body weight. However, this can vary significantly, based on the individual's activity. Additionally, the body requires approximately 8–10 cups of water daily to stay hydrated and function optimally. Individuals need to listen to their body's hunger and thirst signals to provide it with the appropriate amount of nourishment.

In terms of food, the body needs a balanced diet consisting of carbohydrates, proteins, fats, vitamins, minerals, and fibre to function properly and maintain overall health. Carbohydrates provide the body with energy, proteins help build and repair tissues, fats support brain function and hormone production, and vitamins and minerals play essential roles in various bodily processes. Fibre is also important for digestive health and maintaining a healthy weight. It is recommended to consume a variety of nutrient-dense foods in appropriate portion sizes to meet the body's needs. The energy obtained from eating the right kinds of food determines how we respond and perform tasks during the day. Keeping track of our food intake by journalling what we eat and calculating calories helps us monitor daily food consumption.

Additionally, staying adequately hydrated is essential for the body to function properly. Water plays a key role in maintaining body temperature, transporting nutrients and oxygen to cells, removing waste products, and lubricating joints. Dehydration can lead to a range of symptoms such as fatigue, headache, dizziness, and muscle cramps. It is important to drink water consistently throughout the day and pay attention to signs of thirst to ensure that the body remains properly hydrated. Ultimately, understanding the body's needs and providing it with the right amount of food and water is essential for maintaining overall health and well-being.

The quantity of water consumed daily is debatable, and reduced water intake affects the body's ability to expel waste and adequately perform other bodily functions. The formula below determines the quantity of water to drink based on weight and activity level.

1. Consider your weight when determining how much water to drink.
2. Multiply your weight by 2/3 to determine how much water to drink daily. If you weigh 50 kg, the water you need to drink daily is 2/3 of 50, which equals 33 ounces, or less than a litre.
3. Drink 12 ounces of water for every 30 minutes of exercise to replace the fluids lost through sweating. If your workout lasts for 30 minutes, drink an additional

12 ounces of water. So, the total amount of water you need, based on your activity and weight, is 45 ounces or 1.3 litres per day.

Physical Activity

Regular physical activity is essential for maintaining overall health and well-being; thus, finding a balance that works for you is crucial. The amount of daily exercise required varies based on age, fitness level, and health goals. The American Heart Association recommends at least 150 minutes of moderate-intensity aerobic exercise per week for adults, or 75 minutes of vigorous-intensity aerobic exercise. This translates to about 30 minutes per day, five days a week. Additionally, adults should engage in strength training exercises at least two days per week to improve muscle strength and endurance.

However, it is important to note that the recommended amount of exercise may need to be adjusted based on individual factors. For example, highly trained athletes may require more than the standard amount of exercise to maintain their fitness levels. Conversely, individuals with medical conditions may need to consult a healthcare provider to determine a safe and effective exercise regimen. It is also important to listen to your body and adjust accordingly to prevent injury or burnout.

The body releases endorphins—neurotransmitters that act as natural painkillers and mood elevators—in response to stress and physical exertion and are responsible for the feelings of pleasure and euphoria often referred to as the 'runner's high'. Endorphins help mitigate the perception of pain during physical activity, allowing individuals to push their bodies further without feeling discomfort. Additionally, endorphins have been found to reduce stress and anxiety, boost mood, and promote a sense of well-being. This physiological response to exercise encourages individuals to maintain a consistent workout routine and reap the overall health benefits associated with regular physical activity.

The interaction between the body's endorphin system and exercise provides further evidence of the powerful impact that physical activity can have on both physical and mental health, highlighting the importance of incorporating regular exercise for a healthy lifestyle.

Tasks of the Day

Having a daily goal to complete tasks helps individuals prioritise their work and use their time and resources more efficiently. By setting deadlines and milestones for each task, individuals can better manage their workload and ensure that important tasks are completed timely. This not only increases productivity and efficiency, but it also helps individuals build a sense of accomplishment and satisfaction as they work towards achieving their goals.

In the chapter on mindfulness and time management, I will further explore different tools I used to manage my time effectively.

Financial Health

In today's consumerist society, it is more important than ever to be mindful of what we buy. With the constant barrage of advertisements and pressure to keep up with the latest trends, it can be easy to fall into the trap of mindless consumption. However, as responsible citizens of the planet, it is crucial to consider the environmental and ethical implications of our purchasing decisions. By being conscious consumers, we can contribute to a more sustainable world by supporting companies that prioritise environmentally friendly practices and fair labour standards. When considering making a purchase, it is important to ask yourself the following questions:

- Is this item a necessity?
- How will I utilise it once I have acquired it?
- Does it fit within my budget?
- Do I feel confident and in control of my decision?
- Am I purchasing this item solely to impress others?

By reflecting on these inquiries, you can make more informed and thoughtful decisions on your spending habits. Remember to prioritise your needs and financial well-being above external validation. If you purchase an item and later realise that you do not need it, do not dwell on regret. Instead, consider it a valuable learning experience and appreciate the item for what it is.

Social Health

Interactions with others serve as a window into the intricate and multifaceted nature of human relationships. Some interactions leave us feeling invigorated and revitalised, while others drain and deplete us. Despite the emotional ups and downs that accompany these interactions, it is important to acknowledge and appreciate their role in shaping us into better individuals.

Approaching each interaction with a sense of curiosity, humility, and compassion is essential. Recognising that every interaction has the potential to teach us something new about ourselves and the world around us is key. It is crucial to be mindful of our thoughts and emotions during these interactions and to reflect on them later.

When reflecting on our interactions, it is important to ask ourselves some important questions:

- Did I feel understood during the interaction? If not, how can I correct myself without compromising my true self?

- How did I react to challenges or setbacks during the interaction?
- Is there a different approach I could take to handle similar situations in the future?

By being introspective and open to learning from our interactions, we can grow as individuals. Each interaction presents an opportunity for personal growth and self-discovery, and by approaching them with an open mind and a willingness to learn, we can navigate the complexities of human relationships with grace and understanding.

Environmental Health

Waste disposal is a critical issue that impacts communities at both the micro and macro levels. Throwing trash in landfills or oceans can lead to pollution and contamination of air, water, and soil. This can be detrimental to wildlife, marine ecosystems, and human health. For instance, plastic waste in oceans can harm marine animals and disrupt the food chain while hazardous waste in landfills can leach into groundwater, leading to water pollution and potential health risks for nearby communities.

Recycling and proper disposal of waste can help conserve resources, reduce energy consumption, and create economic opportunities through the recycling and repurposing of materials. We can contribute to a healthier environment, a more sustainable economy, and the overall well-being of society By being mindful of how we dispose of waste at an individual level

Another tip for managing waste at an individual level is to compost organic materials. By composting food scraps, yard waste, and other biodegradable materials, we can divert them from landfills where they would otherwise release harmful greenhouse gases as they decompose. Composting not only reduces waste but also creates nutrient-rich soil that can be used in gardens or landscaping.

Before discarding an item, it is important to consider the following questions:

- Can this item be reused?
- Could I have reduced the amount I used in the first place?
- Is this waste recyclable?
- Can I compost this organic waste?

By asking yourself these questions, you can make more environmentally conscious decisions and reduce your overall waste output.

Emotional Health

Some outcomes in our lives result from our choices or decisions and others are just what has been ordained. When these decisions or choices have a positive impact on us or the world around us, we do not stop and think about them. When our decisions result in a negative impact, we often question whether we made the right choice. If we can honestly answer the question, 'Are those decisions in line with my true self?' and feel good about it, then we must have the courage to move forward.

5
What Mindfulness Is Not

'Mindfulness is not a concept it is a practice.'

—Jon Kabat-Zinn

We previously explored and understood mindfulness and the following chapters will speak more of that. However, it is important to understand what mindfulness is not. This is an attempt to break the misconceptions that surround mindfulness. Social media offers a host of information about mindfulness—what it is or is not is relative and based on what we want to achieve by practising mindfulness.

We take on tasks to help us achieve goals we set for ourselves—financial, physical, and sometimes emotional. During this journey to achieve our goals, we are often left with a great sense of overwhelm or anxiety. We then look for ways to overcome the challenges that hinder our journey towards meeting these goals. My mindfulness journey has been all about that. It is a tool that I have used to overcome a sense of overwhelm. It is a lifestyle change that I have adapted to ensure I am aware of every action I take, the reason for my every inaction, and the triggers between me and my goals.

Mindfulness Is Not Absence of Thought

Mindfulness is often misconstrued as a state of mind where thoughts cease to exist. However, this is a fundamental misunderstanding. Mindfulness is the practice of being fully aware of one's thoughts and feelings in the present moment. It involves observing and acknowledging thoughts without judgment or attachment, rather than trying to suppress or eliminate them. Individuals can gain insight into their inner workings and develop greater clarity and control over their mental processes by cultivating this awareness. Thus, mindfulness is not about emptying the mind, rather it is about fully engaging with the richness of one's inner experience.

During a recent word-defining game, a colleague shared an interesting perspective on the colours black and white. She explained that black is the absence of colour while white is the combination of all colours, making it unique in the colour spectrum. For instance, sunlight contains the full spectrum of colours known as VIBGYOR (Violet, Indigo, Blue, Green, Yellow, Orange, and Red), which become visible when light is refracted, creating a rainbow after rainfall.

In the context of mindfulness, it is important to note that striving for a mind devoid of thoughts, akin to the colour black, is a challenging feat, reserved for ascetics. Instead, mindfulness involves acknowledging and accepting both negative and positive thoughts along with the neutral ones, much like the colour white. By cultivating awareness of our thoughts, emotions, and behaviours, we can transcend our fixed mindset and pave the way for personal growth and transformation, much like the creation of a rainbow.

Mindfulness Is Not a Religion

Mindfulness is often mistakenly associated with religion, particularly due to its origins in Buddhist practices. However, mindfulness is secular and is not attached to any religion. It uses tools from different religions and beliefs to help focus on being present in the moment without judgment. It is rooted in psychology and cognitive science principles, emphasising the importance of self-awareness, emotional regulation, and stress reduction. While Buddhist teachings may have influenced mindfulness, it has evolved into a widely recognised therapeutic tool independent of any religious affiliation. Research has shown that mindfulness-based interventions can be effective in treating various mental health issues and improving one's overall well-being, making it accessible and beneficial to individuals of all beliefs and backgrounds.

Researchers have been looking into two different ways to help people be more mindful. The first is called mindfulness-based stress reduction (MBSR), which involves going to group classes once a week and performing mindfulness exercises at home every day for eight weeks. MBSR teaches you how to be more mindful through yoga and meditation. The second method is called mindfulness-based cognitive therapy (MBCT), which combines parts of MBSR with cognitive behavioural therapy (CBT) to help people with depression.

After looking at several studies over the years, researchers have found that mindfulness-based therapy can alleviate stress, anxiety, and depression.

The Pali word '*sati*' (known as '*smriti*' in Sanskrit) is often translated as 'mindfulness', which typically refers to being fully aware and present in the moment. This concept does not conflict with any religious beliefs, as the core principle of any religion is to establish a harmonious relationship with oneself and others to live peacefully.

Embracing this definition, it can be said that mindfulness is aimed at helping individuals be more accepting of themselves and their thoughts as the first step. Mindfulness practice eventually allows individuals to define what brings them joy and tranquillity, empowering them to live a more fulfilling and conscious life.

Mindfulness Is Not Meditation

While mindfulness and meditation are often used interchangeably, it is important to recognise that they are distinct practices. Mindfulness involves being present and fully engaged in the current moment, while meditation is a specific technique used to cultivate mindfulness. Mindfulness can be incorporated into daily activities such as eating, walking, or even washing dishes, whereas meditation typically involves setting aside dedicated time to focus on breathing, thoughts, or bodily sensations. These tools assist in calming the mental chatter.

Mindfulness helps us become more aware of the choices we make daily. What we choose doesn't matter; what matters is how we practice.

Mindfulness Is Not Neglecting Duties

Mindfulness is not about evading responsibilities; it involves facing them with purpose and awareness. As individuals in a connected society, each of us has a unique set of responsibilities that we must fulfil. Mindfulness is not a justification for neglecting these duties. Using retreats to escape from responsibilities under the guise of seeking inner peace is not in alignment with the true essence of mindfulness. While I do not oppose the idea of attending retreats, I do object to using them as a crutch to avoid addressing urgent matters.

The concept that 'mindfulness cannot be used as an excuse to neglect responsibilities' emphasises that while practising mindfulness is beneficial for mental well-being, it should not be misused as a reason to avoid real-life obligations. Evading duties in the name of 'being mindful' can lead to a misunderstanding of what mindfulness truly entails. Mindfulness is not about escaping from life's demands, but rather about approaching them with clarity and calmness. Genuine mindfulness involves being fully present in the moment, even when facing challenges and obligations. It's important to understand that mindfulness is meant to enhance, not replace, active engagement with responsibilities. Therefore, mindfulness should be used to improve accountability, rather than to avoid it.

Mindfulness can help us accomplish our daily goals in an organised manner. When we can collect our thoughts, our daily tasks become more manageable. Mindfulness is commonly associated with being fully present in the moment and focusing on one's thoughts and emotions. By being fully present and attentive to the task at hand, we can approach our duties with a clear and focused mind, leading to improved productivity and better decision-making.

Additionally, mindfulness also teaches us the importance of time management, allowing us to prioritise our tasks effectively. Time management also helps us develop the ability to draw boundaries and learn to embrace conversations and relationships that do not harm us and fill us with immense happiness.

Mindfulness Is Not Relaxation

Mindfulness is often incorrectly equated with relaxation; however, it is important to understand that they are not synonymous. Mindfulness involves intentionally focusing one's attention on the present moment, and being fully aware of thoughts, feelings, sensations, and surroundings without judgment. This requires effort and concentration, which can be quite challenging for individuals not accustomed to being fully present in the moment. While relaxation can be a by-product of mindfulness, it must not be the primary goal.

Individuals can develop greater clarity, insight, and inner calmness through mindfulness. By learning to observe and accept each moment as it arises, individuals can begin to let go of the constant worries and distractions that often plague their minds. As a result, they can experience a deep sense of relaxation and calm cultivated from within. This state of relaxation is not merely a physical sensation, but a mental and emotional state of being that is developed through the intentional habit of mindfulness.

Mindfulness Is Not about Feeling Good All the Time

Mindfulness has become increasingly popular in recent years as a method for managing stress, anxiety, and other challenges in our fast-paced society and is sometimes used as a quick fix—or as it is often called, the 'Buddha pill'. The concept of a 'Buddha pill' might be used critically to describe the oversimplification or commercialisation of spiritual practices, where people seek quick, effortless results rather than engaging deeply with the teachings and practices. It is crucial to understand that mindfulness is not solely about experiencing constant happiness or positivity. It also involves accepting all emotions and sensations that arise—both positive and negative. This is difficult to practise in day-to-day living when we are constantly facing various triggers. It is crucial to recognise that mindfulness is not meant to erase negative feelings or difficult situations, rather it helps individuals develop resilience and a greater sense of self-awareness.

The effects of mindfulness practice are gradual and do not manifest overnight. Simply reading a book on mindfulness or listening to guided meditations will not automatically transform how we communicate with ourselves or interact with the world. Developing a strong mindfulness practice may take different amounts of time for individuals to achieve mental and physical alignment, or to address triggers from relationships.

Through consistent practice, mindfulness enables us to become more attuned to our emotions, physical limitations, and feelings. Acknowledging and addressing these aspects can promote a more harmonious relationship with ourselves and the world around us.

Mindfulness Is Not Easy, but It's Not Difficult Either

Realistic expectations are at the core of success in any endeavour. It is crucial to have realistic expectations to achieve your objectives. Approaching mindfulness with the right mindset is key to reaping its benefits. If you believe mindfulness is easy, you will be disappointed. Conversely, if you view it as challenging, you are setting yourself up for failure before even beginning. Embracing mindfulness with a positive attitude, a clear goal, and a desire to improve yourself will allow you to fully experience and enjoy its benefits for a lifetime.

While the concept of mindfulness may seem simple, it requires a great deal of self-awareness and discipline. Continually bringing oneself back to the present moment and accepting thoughts and feelings as they come can be both challenging and demanding. However, with consistent practise and dedication, mindfulness can be a powerful tool for reducing stress, increasing focus, and improving overall well-being.

Mindfulness Is Not Self-Love but Self-Awareness

Mindfulness is not just a superficial practice of self-love but a profound tool for developing a deep understanding of oneself. It involves observing oneself without judgment or attachment, allowing for a heightened level of self-awareness crucial for personal growth and development. By breaking free from negative patterns and cultivating a deeper understanding and compassion for oneself and others, mindfulness goes beyond mere self-love to truly knowing oneself at a profound level.

While there is much discussion about self-awareness and focusing on one's feelings rather than those of others, it is important to differentiate mindfulness from selfishness. I want to emphasise that there is a clear difference between being selfish and practising self-care. Self-care is a proactive and positive practice aimed at maintaining well-being, while selfishness involves prioritising one's own needs at others' expense. Balancing self-care with empathy and consideration for others is key to fostering healthy relationships and personal satisfaction.

In many contemplative traditions, including Buddhism, the concept of 'self' is considered fluid and not a permanent, unchanging entity. Mindfulness helps us realise this by encouraging us to observe our experiences without attaching them to a solid sense of 'I' or 'me'. Through mindfulness, we become more aware of the transient nature of our thoughts and feelings, which can lead to a deeper understanding that our true essence is not tied to these fleeting experiences. Individuals who practise mindfulness cultivate healthy confidence over time, allowing them to appreciate successes and failures with equanimity.

An example of this growth mindset can be found in the Bhagavad Gita (Chapter 2, Verse 38):

> sukha-duḥkhe same kṛitvā lābhālābhau jayājayau tato
> yuddhāya yujyasva naivaṁ pāpam avāpsyasi.
>
> [Fight for the sake of duty, treating alike happiness and distress, loss and gain, victory and defeat. Fulfilling your responsibility in this way, you will never incur sin.]

This verse encourages individuals to fulfil their responsibilities by treating happiness and distress, loss and gain, victory and defeat with equanimity, ultimately leading to peace and fulfilment.

What you have read thus far is a lot to digest, and I'm sure you have already started scouring the internet on how to get started on your mindfulness journey or are impatient to skip to the next chapters to find out what this book can offer you that you cannot already find on the internet.

While working on this chapter, my mindfulness journey's purpose was challenged, and I felt like I was back in the space where I began this journey. The most fascinating part about mindfulness is the awareness it brings to my triggers. Once I identify them, I can focus on relieving my anxiety. Each starting point may differ, but I always have my tools ready to guide me through these temporary glitches. The challenges we encounter on this path often recur and may appear in new forms each time. However, being on this journey means recognising the right tool for each moment and using it effectively.

I want you, my readers, to perform a few exercises before moving on to the next chapter:

i. Gratitude Exercise: Write down three things you are grateful for that happened today. Remember to thank the universe for something as simple as your breath.
ii. Reflection on Triggers: List two situations that may have triggered you today and analyse how you could have responded differently.
iii. Morning Routine: Set an alarm on your phone to wake you up at a specific time every morning. Place your phone outside your room to encourage a more peaceful start to your day.

You are now ready for the next chapter.

6

General Challenges in Practising Mindfulness

'The only limit to our realisation of tomorrow is our doubts of today.'

—Franklin D. Roosevelt

There can be several reasons mindfulness practice is challenging for many—physical inability due to diseases, mental health issues, lack of goals and discipline, or just simply bad time management. Challenges, whatever they may be and however they may present themselves, the mindfulness journey trains the mind to embrace them without judgment.

According to Patanjali's Yoga Sutras, nine obstacles can prevent one's spiritual routine. Although the challenges expressed in the Patanjali refer to yoga, they can extend to mindfulness, too.

Verse 1:30 of the Yoga Sutra states:

vyādhistyānasanśaya pramādālasyāvirati
bhrāntidarśanālabdha
bhūmikatvānavasthitatvāni
cittavikṣēpāstē'ntarāyāḥ

[Disease, dullness, doubt, carelessness, laziness, worldliness, delusion, non-achievement of a yogic state, and instability are the distractions of the mind and are the obstacles in one's practice.

Vyādhi

Prioritising physical health is essential to fully engage in mindfulness practices. Disease, known as *vyādhi* in Ayurveda, is a common barrier individuals encounter on their journey to achieving optimal health and well-being. Overcoming *vyādhi* necessitates a comprehensive approach that encompasses the physical, mental, and emotional aspects of wellness. Understanding the underlying causes of the disease is crucial in developing a holistic treatment plan that not only addresses the symptoms but also targets the root imbalances within the body.

This treatment plan may involve making lifestyle adjustments, implementing dietary changes, engaging in regular physical activity, practising stress management techniques, and potentially seeking medical intervention. It is important to note that each individual's journey to wellness is unique and may require a personalised approach tailored to their specific needs and circumstances.

By taking a proactive and empowered stance towards their health, individuals can effectively navigate the challenges posed by *vyādhi* and attain optimal well-being. For instance, addressing my GERD issues was a pivotal step before I could fully embrace mindfulness practices such as zero waste, composting, creating household cleaners, and meditation. When the body is in distress, the mind is unable to focus on other tasks.

Styāna

Styāna is a fundamental concept in Hindu philosophy that denotes a state of mental or physical lethargy characterised by an inability to fully engage with tasks or challenges. Overcoming *styāna* necessitates the cultivation of self-awareness, motivation, and effective time management strategies. The key to conquering this state lies in developing a strong sense of purpose and direction, which can aid individuals in remaining focused and driven towards their goals. Additionally, integrating mindfulness and meditation practices can help combat negative thought patterns, promoting mental clarity and presence.

When my daughter was around three years old, my family encountered challenges in motivating her to get out of bed on Monday mornings for school. The weekends were just as hectic as the weekdays, and the commute to school was long. Due to our early work schedules, we had to drop her off at daycare in the morning. To incentivise the children to attend school on Mondays, the school implemented 'Show and Tell Mondays' where children were encouraged to showcase something they were passionate about. This initiative made it easier to wake up my daughter, as having a goal to look forward to gave her motivation and enthusiasm.

Building on that idea, establishing short-term goals can be instrumental in overcoming lethargy. This strategy empowers individuals to break free from complacency and unlock their true potential. Additionally, incorporating breathing exercises and pranayama can significantly improve focus and attention span, assisting individuals in their quest to conquer styāna and attain success. By integrating these practices into daily routines, individuals can effectively combat mental and physical lethargy, ultimately leading to heightened productivity and fulfilment.

Samśaya

In Sanskrit, *samśaya* means doubt or uncertainty. In philosophical and religious contexts, it refers to the feeling of hesitancy or scepticism that arises when faced with complex ideas or conflicting beliefs. Questions like 'Am I doing the right thing?' or 'Am I good enough for this?' often stem from self-doubt, which can be exacerbated by a lack of discipline and poor time management.

Overcoming this doubt and uncertainty can be challenging, requiring self-reflection, resilience, and determination. To overcome self-doubt, individuals must first identify the reasons behind their uncertainties, if they arise from past experiences, external influences, or internal insecurities. Through mindfulness meditation or journalling, individuals can also gain insight into their thoughts and feelings, allowing them to challenge any negative beliefs contributing to their doubts. Building a support network of friends, family, or mentors can provide encouragement and guidance, helping individuals navigate moments of uncertainty. Setting small, achievable goals and celebrating success can boost confidence and motivation, leading to a greater sense of self-assurance and security.

Pramādā

In Hindu philosophy, *pramādā* is defined as negligence or carelessness, particularly concerning spiritual practices and self-discipline. It is believed that it can impede one's progress on the journey to self-realisation and enlightenment. *Pramādā* can manifest as procrastination, lack of focus, or failure to engage in tasks.

Carelessness often arises from a mind that is constantly distracted, leading to an indifferent attitude towards achieving goals. This can develop into a harmful habit as individuals may easily resort to taking shortcuts.

By being mindful of *pramādā* and actively working to overcome it, one can develop self-discipline, enhance productivity, and ultimately achieve success in both spiritual and academic pursuits. It is essential to recognise and address *pramādā* to progress towards personal growth and fulfilment.

Alasyā

The concept of *alasyā* pertains to a state of laziness or inactivity that hinders spiritual growth and enlightenment. *Alasyā* is seen as a barrier to progress on the path of self-realisation as it hampers individuals from fulfilling their duties and participating in activities that boost personal development. With laziness, a feeling of heaviness also sets in, making it challenging to muster the motivation to take necessary actions. This pattern can lead to, what is commonly known as, depression.

Encouraging someone in this state to partake in physical activity or energy-boosting exercises can be daunting. Seeking assistance and integrating simple meditation practices, such as nature walks or seated meditation, can prove beneficial in overcoming this state of inertia.

Avirati

This concept emphasises the importance of self-discipline and self-control in leading a virtuous and enlightened life. Through *avirati*, individuals strive to detach themselves from the distractions that can cloud their moral judgment and hinder their spiritual growth. An excessive preoccupation with worldly cravings and desires can divert attention from the ultimate goal. Whether it is an insatiable craving for sweets, substance abuse, or an overwhelming desire to shop—self-discipline and consistent practise of asanas that target and mitigate this excessive and detrimental energy are essential for control.

Managing sweet cravings can be a challenge for many, including my family. While we make a conscious effort to not overindulge in sweets, we take proactive steps to keep our cravings in check. One key strategy is identifying triggers that spark cravings. By recognising these triggers, we can work on avoiding them and find healthier ways to manage them.

Maintaining a well-balanced diet and staying hydrated are also crucial in controlling cravings. Consuming nutrient-rich meals with plenty of fibre can help stabilise blood sugar levels and prevent sudden urges for sweets. Additionally, staying hydrated throughout the day is important as dehydration can sometimes be mistaken for hunger.

Bhrāntidarśanā

Also known as delusion in Sanskrit, *bhrāntidarśanā* refers to a state of distorted perception or belief that is not grounded in reality. In philosophical terms, it signifies a misunderstanding of the true nature of existence and the self. This concept holds significant importance in Indian philosophy, particularly within the realm of spiritual practice and the pursuit of enlightenment. *Bhrāntidarśanā* can manifest in various forms—attachment to material possessions, identification with the ego, or holding onto false ideas about the nature of the world. It is widely recognised as a hindrance to spiritual growth and must be overcome through self-awareness, mindfulness, and the pursuit of knowledge.

Humans have a natural inclination towards seeking validation for the stories they tell themselves. Often, individuals surround themselves with people who validate their emotions rather than challenge them. When faced with challenges to their beliefs, individuals may feel threatened and go to great lengths to avoid such confrontations, even at the cost of losing valuable relationships. The narratives we construct for ourselves serve as the foundation for our actions and decisions. When these narratives are distorted, they can obstruct personal, professional, and spiritual growth.

Seeking professional assistance can be instrumental in dispelling these illusions and alleviating feelings of despair. By doing so, individuals can move forward with clarity and purpose, enabling them to overcome obstacles and achieve their full potential.

Alabdhabhūmikatvā

This refers to the state of being unable to achieve one's desired objectives or goals due to external or internal obstacles. This concept speaks to the idea that despite one's efforts and intentions, there are factors beyond one's control that may hinder success.

When faced with obstacles, it is important to approach them with a strategic and proactive mindset. Keeping the goal in mind is imperative in overcoming obstacles. When my family and I faced different challenges over and over again, the steps we took were as such:

a. Identify the specific challenge and analyse its root causes.
b. Create a detailed action plan outlining achievable steps towards overcoming it. Determine the kind of resources you can leverage to help you overcome the challenge. For example, will getting a temporary house help alleviate the challenge? Will meeting experts in that field provide more insight? Will speaking to others, who have been in similar situations, help you understand the options better?
c. Maintain a positive attitude and stay resilient in the face of setbacks as perseverance is key to navigating through difficulties.
d. Finally, continuously evaluate and do a sanity check on where you are with overcoming those obstacles and adjust your strategies as needed to ensure that you are on track towards success.

Alabdhabhūmikatvā serves as a reminder that setbacks are a natural part of the learning process. Ultimately, this concept highlights the significance of patience, self-reflection, and adaptability in pursuing goals.

Anavasthitatvā

This concept challenges the notion of relying on material objects or external sources for a sense of permanence or stability, as everything in the material world is subject to change and impermanence. *Anavasthitatvā* encourages individuals to look within themselves for completeness and truth, rather than seeking validation or security from external sources.

In today's materialistic society, it is easy to fall into the trap of placing excessive value on material objects. One effective way to overcome reliance on material objects is to practise the 3Rs—reduce, reuse, and recycle. By reducing the consumption of material goods we can minimise our dependency on these possessions. This involves being mindful of what we purchase and only buying what we truly need. Reusing items instead of immediately discarding them can prolong their lifespan and reduce waste. Developing a habit of recycling helps in conserving resources and minimising environmental impact. By incorporating these principles into our daily lives, we can cultivate a more sustainable mindset and reduce our attachment to physical possessions. This approach not only benefits the environment but also promotes a more minimalist lifestyle focused on experiences rather than belongings.

My primary goal in embracing this journey of mindfulness is to ensure that every step I take is done with complete awareness. I believe the generation before mine is living their golden years with a lot of regret, and I do not want that for myself or my family. I want to ensure that the richest legacy I pass on to my child is that of demonstrating how to live an authentic life devoid of regrets. I want to take every step or make every move with awareness.

The biggest challenge that I face in my mindfulness journey is generational trauma. I am at constant odds between my inner child, who wants to or has been accustomed to behaving in a particular way, and the present me, who feels those ways may not apply to me or the generations that follow. I am a work-in-progress, but I know I have come a long way. I seek resilience to stay on the authentic path I have carved for myself.

7
Embracing Mindfulness during Difficult Times

'Into each life some rain must fall . . .'

—Henry Wadsworth Longfellow

Longfellow's insight still holds true: Everyone encounters dark and challenging times. These difficult moments undoubtedly provide valuable lessons. It is only after overcoming these challenges that we can reflect on how the situation was handled and consider ways to improve our resilience through mindfulness practices.

Mindfulness techniques like guided meditation and breathwork have been proven effective, but the question is, how can one embrace these practices during hardship? How can one transition from high-stress situations to incorporating meditation when there are pressing issues demanding one's attention? The key lies in creating pockets of space for yourself amidst the chaos. These moments can be found before bed, during a bath, while cooking, eating, or even walking.

First and foremost, it is important to recognise that whatever you are experiencing is temporary, and this phase does not define your entire life. Remember that things will improve, and when you look back on the current situation, you should feel proud of how you navigated it.

BEAT ™ (a term I coined) the stress and anxiety with this technique. When you feel overwhelmed by an emotion, try this technique:

1. **B**reathe in and breathe out and focus on the breath. Use the physiological sigh or other breathing techniques mentioned in Chapter 12 that you think can help you. This will help your body understand that you are trying to regulate your emotions.
2. **E**valuate the extent to which the anxious thoughts are causing you pain. If you are in physical pain, seek help to ensure that your pain is manageable. If you feel emotional pain and think you need help, immediately reach out to someone you trust. Once the pain or situation is manageable for you, move on to the next step.
3. **A**nalyse or accept the source of your triggers. Determine if it is a physical trigger that you can address, such as hunger, pain, intense heat or cold, or an emotional cause. If you can move away from that or alleviate it, then do so, or minimise the interactions with the triggers. If none of these work and the situation remains the same, understand that there is no way out of this other than accepting the circumstances and developing resilience to bear with what you are going through.
4. **T**reat this phase and give it the due attention it needs. Sometimes it doesn't just rain like Longfellow proposed but pours. Sometimes, difficulties do not take turns; they have a domino effect. Other times, they arise all at once. Thus, prioritise and perform your tasks by the order of importance, ticking them off one at a time. If you need help, do not hesitate to ask for it. If there is too much on your plate, delegate. Slowly but surely the tasks will be completed, and the problems will be solved. Ultimately, the sun always rises.

Journal your thoughts if you can. Practise breathwork while walking, cooking, before sleeping, or when you are in pain. Acknowledging pain makes us kinder to ourselves.

8

Healing: It Runs in the Family

'The past is never where you think you left it.'
—Michael Ondaatje

'It runs in the family . . .' is a phrase we may have heard often that denotes traits, behaviours, or habits that get passed on from one generation to another. Bethany Webster's writing on 'Mother Wound' was a huge revelation for me. All that my mother went through in trying to make her marriage a success in the eyes of society, what my grandmother would have gone through in her way and her ancestors, too, came racing to my mind. My first thought was that I must not pass my unhealed thoughts on to my daughter. Epigenetics, the study of how your behaviours and environment can cause changes to the way your genes work, has enough evidence to prove how strong feelings—negative or positive—can easily pass on to the next generation. According to a native Indian saying, 'Healing oneself, will ensure that seven generations before and after you are healed.'

Success is not limited to financial wealth. It also involves gaining a wealth of knowledge and happiness through successful relationships. Healing the ancestral trauma ensures that not only will our ancestors be at peace, but future generations will also not be burdened with the dysregulated emotions that we may, knowingly or unknowingly, carry on from our ancestors.

Actionable Ways to Heal Your Lineage

The suggestions provided here are what has proven effective for me as I navigate my emotions. I am dedicated to cultivating a more compassionate relationship with myself and embracing my fears and limitations with grace and understanding. This continuous journey of self-discovery and personal growth has equipped me to face life's challenges with resilience and authenticity.

I find this verse from the Bhagavad Gita (Chapter 6, Verse 35) particularly relevant:

> *Śhrī bhagavān uvācha*
>
> *asanśhayaṁ mahā-bāho mano durnigrahaṁ chalam*
>
> *abhyāsena tu kaunteya vairāgyeṇa cha gṛihyate*
>
> [Lord Krishna said: O mighty-armed son of Kunti, what you say is correct; the mind is very difficult to restrain. But by practise and detachment, it can be controlled.]

Lofty thoughts . . . however, how can one put them into action? Simply by taking baby steps and embracing the philosophy that every person in this world is born alone and will die alone. These relationships, formed during our journey of life, are tools or experiences that help us become better human beings. The goal of a psychotherapist is to ensure you feel empowered with your emotions. Seeking professional help to understand the attachment styles each of us possess, not only with ourselves but with others as well, can allow us to stop seeking validation for our actions.

Accept Your Emotions

When seeking to free the mind from a painful experience, it is crucial to first acknowledge and accept the emotions tied to the event. This may involve allowing oneself to experience pain, anger, or sadness without passing judgment. A simple technique that I use when I am acknowledging my emotion is to tap on my chest—like in the movie *3 Idiots*—and say, 'All is well.' For, it would be well. Emotions come and go. Greet them or bid them farewell as they enter or exit your thoughts, like a train arriving at its platform or departing from it.

I found solace and inspiration in the enlightening podcasts of influential figures such as Guru Gaur Gopal Das, Swami Dayananda Saraswathi, Swami Chinmayananda, Jay Shetty, Bethany Webster, and Gabby Bernstein during my daily walks. Additionally, Michelle Obama's book *The Light We Carry: Overcoming in Uncertain Times* significantly shifted my perspective and nurtured self-acceptance, resonating with me.

Through the wisdom imparted by these influencers, I gained a deeper understanding of my attachment style in relationships. As I continue to grow and evolve, I can proudly affirm that through continuing mindfulness practice, I have cultivated a deeper sense of self-compassion that helps me address an issue in my mind in all honesty and with more kindness.

Understand the Subtle Dynamics

We live in a society where individuals rely on each other for support and encouragement, often aligning with each other's perspectives. However, when certain circumstances lead to a departure from this interconnected society, like a job change, relocation to a different country, or marrying into a family with a different culture, it is important to recognise that others may not fully understand your thinking.

While others can empathise with us, it may be more beneficial for our mental health to not expect them to have a complete understanding of our thoughts and actions. It is important to stay true to oneself and remain steadfast on the path of truth.

The challenges we face are not always visible to those around us. There have been numerous instances where I longed for my perspective to be acknowledged, only to realise that people will perceive things as they wish and see my actions only from their perspective. I am reminded of a quote by Chitra Bannerjee from her book *The Palace of Illusions*, 'Isn't that what truth is? The force of a person's believing steps into those around him—into the very earth and air and water—until there is nothing else.'

Throughout my journey, I have experienced a profound transformation in my understanding of love, family, and relationships. I have learnt that, at the end of the day, everyone is an individual who operates from a space of survival or a need to be heard. It may be my parents whose survival depended on those around them who could help them physically, my colleagues, who felt the need to be louder so they could be heard better, or it could even be me, who chose to take action to remain authentic to myself. Whatever it may be, I realise now that every reaction and response of an individual takes root from the desire to create a space in the universe they can call their own.

As I continue this journey of self-discovery and growth, I am committed to facing these challenges head-on and working towards a deeper understanding of love, family dynamics, and healthy relationships.

Practise Gratitude

I am grateful for the positive and negative life experiences as they have motivated me to prioritise self-improvement and strive for personal growth. Acknowledging the uniqueness of each individual and their struggles, I have actively worked to break the cycle of trauma within my family. As we transitioned from a close-knit unit to a more fragmented one, I recognised the significance of addressing these issues to prevent their perpetuation in future generations.

Taking Responsibility

I do not attribute my shortcomings to my ancestors or forefathers. I take full responsibility for my flaws and experiences as they are a direct result of the choices I have made. However, it is important to recognise that our choices and thought patterns are greatly influenced by our childhood experiences, leading to the ongoing debate of nature versus nurture. By developing an awareness of our emotions, feelings, actions, and choices, we can navigate through life more effectively. It is essential to reframe our education and experiences to find fulfilment in our pursuits without constantly seeking external validation.

Be Kind to Yourself

Being kind to yourself is key to maintaining mental and emotional well-being, especially in high-pressure work environments. It involves treating yourself with compassion, understanding, and forgiveness. We often hold ourselves to high standards and push ourselves to achieve goals, sometimes at the expense of our self-care. Through self-compassion and kindness towards ourselves, we can prevent burnout, reduce stress levels, and improve overall productivity. Instead of dwelling on our shortcomings, acknowledging our accomplishments allows us to build self-confidence and resilience in the face of challenges. By cultivating a growth mindset and showing ourselves the same empathy we extend towards others, we can foster a healthier work environment and maintain peak performance in our professional endeavours.

Seek Help

Seeking support from a therapist or counsellor can offer valuable guidance and perspective on how to process and overcome a painful experience. Emotions are intricate and can be influenced by various internal and external factors. It is essential to recognise that managing emotions is a skill that requires time and practise to develop. Overcoming emotional challenges necessitates introspection, self-compassion, and, at times, seeking professional assistance or guidance.

Journal Stories of Ancestral Behaviour

Management expert Peter Drucker once famously said, 'You can't manage what you can't measure.' This principle is widely recognised in the world of business management and holds true when it comes to managing behavioural change as well.

To begin the process of self-improvement, it is important to reflect on the positive and negative characteristics of your ancestors you wish to either adopt or change within yourself. This exercise should be approached with a mindset of self-awareness and a desire to positively impact future generations. By identifying these traits, you can better understand your behaviour and work towards personal growth and development.

Thank Your Ancestors

Our present circumstances are a direct result of the sacrifices, hard work, and prayers of our ancestors. Without their contributions, we would not be where we are today. It is important to acknowledge and appreciate the positive traits that have been passed down to us by our ancestors. If they are still alive, take the time to express your gratitude to them. If they have passed on or if your relationship does not allow for such communication, consider writing a thank you note and placing it in a gratitude jar.

Gratitude is cultivated when we acknowledge our emotions, forgive ourselves, and release negative feelings towards others. A poignant quote by author Karen Salmansohn comes to mind:

> The time has come to forgive your parents.
> For all things.

Big.
And small.
You must recognise that they were coming from a place of limitations.
Promise yourself that you won't let their limitations create limitations within you.
Be aware of what has happened in your past.
Shed that light upon it, so you can see it clearly.
Acknowledge it all.
Then let it go.
Your light is better spent aimed at all that is wonderful about you and the present life you are creating for yourself.

Draw Boundaries with Your Ancestors

It is crucial to express gratitude towards our ancestors for who we are and what we have achieved. However, it is equally important to establish boundaries when we encounter unresolved issues within our ancestral lineage that we are not equipped to address. While this approach may not align with certain cultural norms and could be perceived as impolite, it is essential for our well-being.

Be compassionate yet assertive in setting boundaries with your ancestors. If attempts to communicate and address these issues are met with resistance or lack of understanding, seeking professional guidance to navigate effective communication strategies may prove beneficial. Find ways to deal with their inner child issues. For instance, if the parents show signs of anxiety as an unresolved trauma, gently but firmly address that by giving them enough information within the limits of your comfort. Remember, prioritising your mental and emotional health is paramount in this process.

What are you waiting for? Start your journalling today! Write down whatever is on your mind. If you are unable to, then at the very least start with what emotions you feel.

9
Exploring the World through the Lens of Mindfulness

'The journey of life is not a journey from one place to another, but a journey from ignorance to wisdom.'
—Socrates

Mindfulness practices are prevalent in various religions and cultures across the globe, each with its unique approach to cultivating a sense of awareness and presence. As an expatriate, I have had a unique experience of living in countries that embrace different religious beliefs. Although most countries I have lived in have a diverse population and are home to a wide variety of religions, they embrace a predominant religion with the majority of the population identifying with it.

Mindfulness practices in different religions and religions promote inner peace, self-awareness, and spiritual growth. Regardless of religious differences, mindfulness techniques share the common goal of fostering clarity, compassion, and gratitude in individuals' lives by promoting a deeper connection to oneself, others, and the divine.

Indian Traditions, Childhood Habits, and Mindfulness

I was born and raised in India and so was my husband. Both of us were exposed to the rich cultural heritage and diversity of our country from a young age, which shaped our worldviews and values. Our upbringing in India instilled a deep sense of community, respect for traditions, and a strong work ethic in us. These experiences have greatly influenced our perspective on life, relationships, and success.

For many, including my husband and I, growing up in India, mindfulness is not an abstract concept but a practical tool used in everyday life. From crossing a crowded road to navigating the complexities of social interactions, these experiences train us to remain alert, aware, and composed.

Crossing a crowded road, for instance, in India requires a high level of attentiveness and presence. The constant flow of traffic, pedestrians, and unpredictable elements like animals or vendors demand that one stays fully aware of the surroundings. This situation naturally fosters mindfulness, as it requires being in the moment, anticipating movements, and responding calmly and swiftly.

In environments like those in India, mindfulness is not just a practice but a survival skill. The ability to stay calm, focused, and adaptable amidst chaos is crucial. Indian streets, with their blend of unpredictability and diversity, teach people to embrace uncertainty with a mindful attitude.

Beyond simply crossing the road, Indian culture places a strong emphasis on being fully engaged in daily activities due to its many moving parts. This is evident in rituals, family interactions, and community life, which encourage being present and attentive, reinforcing mindfulness.

While it is an overstatement to claim that everyone born in India can easily adapt to mindfulness given its population of over 1.4 billion, it's safe to say that those raised in India for most of their lives find it easier to embrace mindfulness. They are not only exposed to and surrounded by yoga, ayurveda, and various disciplines that promote mindfulness but are also inherently equipped with the tools to manage changes.

Canada, Native Indian Beliefs, and Mindfulness

Canada is renowned for its cultural diversity, prompting my family to decide to immigrate in pursuit of better opportunities. The country's reputation as a melting pot of cultures proved true as we were warmly embraced by a myriad of ethnic groups and traditions. This inclusivity can enhance mindfulness by encouraging individuals to be more aware of and sensitive to different experiences and backgrounds.

Canadians are often noted for their politeness and respect for others. This cultural norm encourages mindful communication—being present and considerate in interactions, listening attentively, and responding thoughtfully. Such practices align closely with the principles of mindfulness, which include awareness and non-judgment in relationships.

During our time in Canada, we had numerous opportunities to engage with individuals from various walks of life and cultural backgrounds. One memorable encounter was with my husband's colleague, who hailed from a Native Indian heritage. As we conversed, I discovered we shared a mutual interest in culture and traditions. It was through her that I learnt about the concept of healing ourselves to heal seven generations before and after us. She eloquently expounded on this philosophy and shared how her faith and embracing religious beliefs had helped her overcome many challenges.

Thais, Creativity, and Mindfulness

Thailand is known for its rich cultural heritage and diverse religious landscape. While Buddhism is the predominant religion in Thailand, with approximately 95 per cent of the population identifying as Buddhist, the country also features a significant Muslim minority along with smaller populations of Christians, Hindus, and practitioners of Indigenous folk religions. The unique blend of religious traditions in Thailand is reflected in the country's architecture, art, and daily life, with Buddhist temples and shrines coexisting alongside mosques and churches. This religious diversity underscores Thailand's reputation as a tolerant and accepting society, where different faiths can peacefully live and contribute to the country's vibrant cultural tapestry.

One of the most well-known religions that incorporates mindfulness practices is Buddhism. In Buddhism, mindfulness is central to meditation and is seen as a means to achieve enlightenment. Mindfulness in Buddhism involves focusing on the present moment, observing one's thoughts and emotions without judgment, and cultivating a sense of compassion and acceptance towards oneself and others.

Reflecting on my mindfulness journey, Thailand played a significant role in shaping my perspective. The people of Thailand left a lasting impression on me as their artistic nature and appreciation for the simple things in life were truly inspiring. Immersing myself in the Thai language was essential during my time there, as it allowed me to connect more deeply with my colleagues and the local culture.

The contrast between Thai culture and North America—from where we moved—was eye-opening, teaching me to slow down and find joy in the little moments. It was in Thailand that I found the inspiration to compile my thoughts and publish my first book, *Shells on The Beach*.

In many cultures, the concept of hospitality plays a crucial role in social interactions. One such example is the Thai expression '*sawadika*', which is commonly used to greet others and convey a sense of warmth and welcome. The tradition of saying *sawadika* reminds us of the importance of kindness and openness in our interactions with others, ultimately contributing to a more inclusive and harmonious society. I am grateful for the kindness and warmth with which the Thai people welcomed me and my family, introducing me to the loving-kindness meditation. Thailand will always hold a special place in my heart as a pivotal moment in my mindfulness journey.

Dubai, Contemplation, and Mindfulness

During our time as expatriates in Dubai, we were immersed in a city where Islam reigns as the predominant religion, with the majority of the population identifying as Muslim. The city is adorned with numerous mosques where worshippers gather for prayers and communal activities. However, Dubai is also home to significant populations of Hindus, Christians, Sikhs, Buddhists, and other faiths. Hindu temples like the Shiva Temple and Gurudwaras such as Guru Nanak Darbar cater to the spiritual needs of these diverse communities. The city's religious diversity is further showcased through its various churches, synagogues, and places of worship for other faiths. Dubai's commitment to religious tolerance and freedom allows individuals from different backgrounds to practise their beliefs openly and peacefully within the boundaries of the law.

One of the most unique experiences we had during our time in Dubai was being invited to an Iftar dinner with an Emirati during the holy month of Ramadan. This cultural experience provided us with a deep understanding of Emirati customs and traditions. The evening began with a traditional Iftar dinner followed by a visit to a local mosque.

Iftar is the evening meal during Ramadan when Muslims break their fast. It is a time for friends and family to come together, fostering a sense of unity and family connections. Sharing a meal during Iftar allows for the exchange of ideas and emotions, reinforcing family values.

The dinner was elegantly presented on low-lying tables placed atop exquisite hand-woven carpets. The table setting followed a traditional Arabic style, and we were respectfully asked to observe silence during the prayer. Following the prayer, the fast was broken with Arabic coffee and dates, leading into a feast of traditional Arabic cuisine including falafel, hummus, bread, tabouleh, and other delicacies. Each bite was savoured, allowing us to appreciate the rich flavours and cultural significance of the meal.

During our tour of the mosque, we had the opportunity to observe the prayers being conducted. Following this, we engaged in an open discussion regarding Emirati culture and traditions. My curiosity and interest in various religions prompted me to ask numerous questions about Islamic teachings. The Emirati guide graciously answered all my inquiries, leading to a fruitful discussion on the significance of these teachings.

Interestingly, our conversation inspired me to reflect on the role of mindfulness in Islamic religions. Within Islamic teachings, there is a strong emphasis on connecting with Allah through prayer, contemplation, and meditation. Practices such as deep breathing, focusing on the present moment, and cultivating gratitude closely align with Islamic principles of *tawakkul* (trust in Allah), *sabr* (patience), and *shukr* (gratitude). Muslims, knowingly or unknowingly, deepen their spiritual connection to Allah by engaging in a variety of mindfulness practices.

The United Kingdom, Gratitude, and Mindfulness

Upon relocating to the United Kingdom, I was presented with several unique opportunities to engage with the ever-so-courteous British people and immerse myself in British culture.

British culture is renowned for its emphasis on politeness, patience, and consideration for others. These social norms align with the principles of mindfulness, which involve being aware of others, actively listening, and responding thoughtfully. The focus on courteous behaviour can cultivate mindfulness in interactions, enabling individuals to be present and respectful in their communication. We had very patient neighbours while living in London, and we are deeply grateful for that opportunity to experience kind humans like them.

We were also fortunate to immerse ourselves in the rich history and cultural heritage of Britain, which provide opportunities for reflection and a deeper understanding of the human experience. This cultural immersion led to increased self-awareness and a realisation of the transient nature of life, both integral aspects of mindfulness.

As with any Western culture, British culture also places importance on privacy and personal space. This respect for boundaries can promote mindfulness by encouraging individuals to prioritise self-care, engage in introspection, and be mindful of their own needs and emotions, as well as those of others.

I vividly recall, during my visit to St Paul's Cathedral, I was privileged to attend Mass conducted by one of the priests. The priest emphasised the importance of acceptance as the cornerstone of happiness, suggesting that it can be attained through contemplation or prayer.

While at the cathedral, I encountered an elderly lady struggling to ascend the stairs. I offered my assistance, and in return, she imparted a profound piece of wisdom: 'Climbing up is always more difficult than climbing down, but the joy of reaching the top far surpasses that of descending to the bottom.' This statement resonated with me deeply. Later, as we conversed over a cup of tea (that the British love), the elderly lady shared her thoughts on various topics, ranging from her sadness about the infrequent visits with her grandchildren to her allergies and, naturally, how religion and her daily practices, such as gardening and visiting the church, has helped her cope with her challenges for over 85 years. It was fascinating to draw parallels between Hinduism and Christianity, ultimately realising that both religions share a common goal of connecting with the divine, fostering gratitude, and maintaining humility despite life's challenges.

France, Nature, and Mindfulness

French culture emphasises quality of life, appreciation for art and beauty, and a slower pace of living, offering several avenues to support and enhance mindfulness practice.

One significant aspect of French culture is the value placed on food and dining. Meals in France are seen as an experience to be savoured rather than rushed. The French practice of eating slowly, appreciating flavours, and engaging in meaningful conversation during meals encourages mindfulness. During my time in France, my culinary exploration reached a more creative level. Every dinner we hosted became a 'Michelin Experience', as our guests would say. My mind naturally chose creativity to engage my senses more productively. Despite facing many challenges with my husband's career during those years in France, I am grateful for the creative opportunities that I experienced while living in France.

France has a deep appreciation for art, beauty, and aesthetics, from its world-renowned museums and architecture to fashion and design. This cultural focus on appreciating beauty encourages mindfulness by inviting us to observe and enjoy the finer details of life.

French culture values work-life balance, with a strong emphasis on leisure time, family, and personal well-being. The legal structure supports this with generous vacation time (30 days per year) and shorter workweeks, allowing French residents more opportunities to relax, reflect, and engage in mindful activities.

France's diverse landscapes, from the rolling countryside to the Mediterranean coast and Alpine regions, offer ample opportunities for outdoor activities. The French often take time to enjoy nature through hiking, picnicking, or simply strolling through parks and gardens. This connection to nature promotes mindfulness by encouraging individuals to be present and appreciate the natural world.

Our time in France was truly transformative, providing invaluable insights and lessons that significantly enriched my personal growth. France is renowned for its stunning landscapes and diverse terrain, featuring vast expanses of lush greenery and numerous water bodies scattered throughout the countryside. These peaceful settings offer a welcome escape from the hustle and bustle of city life, allowing residents to reconnect with nature.

During our stay in a charming village nestled within this expansive country, I had the opportunity to immerse myself in all the natural surroundings and generously shared their joy with us. Engaging with nature has allowed me to practise mindfulness in a way that has positively impacted my life. By fully embracing the sights, sounds, and rhythms of the natural world, I enhanced my focus, attention, and overall well-being. Taking leisurely walks along the River Seine and its tributaries enabled me to disconnect from the distractions of technology and modern life, allowing me to be fully present in the moment.

The rejuvenating power of nature has proven to be an invaluable tool for self-care and personal development. I can confidently attest that embracing nature has fostered a greater sense of clarity, purpose, and resilience in my life.

As I reflect on my journey through life and as I write this, like most of us, I am uncertain where it may lead me. However, I am certain of my commitment to embracing and accepting all opportunities that come my way with open arms. I am determined to approach every challenge as a valuable learning experience.

Each day, I recite the Serenity Prayer as a reminder of my values and beliefs: 'God, grant me the serenity to accept the things I cannot change, the courage to change the things I can, and the wisdom to know the difference.' This prayer serves as a guiding principle in my life, helping me navigate the joys and struggles that come my way.

10
The Timeless Wisdom of Ancient Practices

'We are bound to our ancestors and to those who made us, whether we want to be or not. What matters is what we make of what we are.'

—Kate Elliott

Our forefathers possessed great wisdom in incorporating rituals and habits into their daily lives. This required immense dedication and perseverance to establish these rituals as part of their daily routine. To ensure adherence to these practices, they often intertwined them with religious beliefs and rituals, instilling a deep sense of reverence and fear of God.

By incorporating ritualistic practices passed down by our ancestors, we can cultivate a sense of tranquillity and focus in our daily lives. This connection to our heritage promotes a feeling of belonging and enhances our ability to concentrate on the tasks at hand. Embracing mindfulness through ancestral rituals can lead to a more grounded and purposeful existence in today's world.

The timeless wisdom of ancient practices refers to the wealth of knowledge and insights passed down through generations from various cultures and traditions. These ancient routines, rooted in various cultures and belief systems, offer valuable insights into the human experience and guidance for living a more balanced and fulfilling life. These practices encompass a wide range of disciplines including but not limited to meditation, yoga, acupuncture, herbal medicine, and t'ai chi. These have stood the test of time because they are grounded in universal principles that apply to all individuals. By incorporating these ancient practices into our modern lifestyles, we can tap into a wealth of wisdom cultivated over centuries and find solutions to many of the challenges we face today. By honouring and embracing these traditions, we can improve our well-being and preserve the cultural heritage and collective knowledge.

The enduring appeal of these ancient practices lies in their ability to promote holistic well-being by uniting the mind, body, and spirit. Several studies have shown that incorporating even a few elements of these customs into one's daily routine can lead to reduced stress levels, improved mental clarity, increased physical strength and flexibility, and enhanced emotional resilience.

According to a 2016 study by Gemma Perry, Professor Bill Thompson, and Dr Vince Polito, practising the universal chant 'Om' for just 10 minutes showed improvements in one's attention levels, a more positive emotional state, and increased feelings of connectedness among individuals.[1]

In traditional South Indian households, mindfulness practices were abundant in daily routines in ancient times. The day would commence with the ritual of clearing the surroundings and creating a *kolam* with rice flour, not only for aesthetic purposes but also to feed the ants. Mindfulness was then integrated into various activities throughout the day, such as cooking, eating, waste segregation, and tending to the Tulsi plant. While the fast-paced nature of modern life may hinder the exact replication of these practices, the

1. Gemma Perry, Vince Polito, and William Forde Thompson, '*Chanting Meditation Improves Mood and Social Cohesion*' (2016).

desire to embrace mindfulness can still be fulfilled by following ancestral traditions.

Superstitions have often been viewed as irrational beliefs or practices stemming from cultural traditions and folklore. However, some scholars argue that superstitions may have served a practical purpose in instilling mindfulness among individuals. People were reminded to pay closer attention to their surroundings, behaviours, and actions by adhering to superstitions. This heightened awareness led to a more cautious and deliberate approach to decision-making, ultimately promoting mindfulness in daily activities. For instance, the belief in avoiding walking under ladders may have encouraged individuals to be mindful of potential dangers above them.

Superstitions can also be seen as methods of cultivating mindfulness by prompting individuals to think critically about their actions and surroundings. It is essential to delve deeper into the rationale behind these customs, seeking logical and scientific explanations to dispel any notion of superstition.

Adapting Ancient Wisdom to Contemporary Lifestyles

In today's fast-paced and ever-changing world, there is a growing interest in adapting ancient wisdom to contemporary lifestyles as a means of finding balance and fulfilment.

Mindfulness meditation, yoga, and traditional medicine have been valued for centuries for their abilities to promote holistic health, resilience, and well-being. In a study conducted by Seng Oh et al., 2022, it was found that mindfulness played an intervening role for enhanced psychological well-being in building the leave of resilience.[2] Incorporating ancient mindfulness practices into our modern lives doesn't require retreating to a mountaintop. By integrating these ancient

2. Vincent Kim Seng Oh, Abdullah Sarwar, and Niaz Pervez, '*The Study of Mindfulness as an Intervening Factor for Enhanced Psychological Well-Being in Building the Level of Resilience*' (2022).

teachings into our modern lives through our daily routines, we can cultivate greater self-awareness, reduce stress, and improve our overall quality of life.

Even in a professional setting, as organisations increasingly recognise the importance of employee well-being in driving success, the integration of ancient practices into workplace culture has become a strategic priority.

Physical Benefits

Ancient teachings on mindfulness offer a treasure trove of physical benefits. These practices help cultivate a deeper connection between the mind and body, promoting overall physical well-being. By intentionally focusing on the present moment, individuals practising mindful living can reduce stress levels, lower blood pressure, and alleviate symptoms of chronic illnesses such as heart disease and diabetes. Additionally, by being fully present in their daily activities—eating nutritious meals, exercising regularly, and getting adequate rest—individuals are more likely to make healthy lifestyle choices that benefit their overall well-being.

Autoimmune disorders are characterised by the body's immune system mistakenly attacking its own cells, leading to chronic inflammation and tissue damage. Recent research suggests that mindfulness practices like meditation and deep breathing exercises may help reduce symptoms and improve overall health in individuals with autoimmune disorders[3]. Mindfulness has also been shown to decrease stress levels, which can trigger or exacerbate autoimmune responses. By

3. Leina S. Alrabadi et al. 'Mindfulness-Based Stress Reduction May Decrease Stress, Disease Activity, and Inflammatory Cytokine Levels in Patients with Autoimmune Hepatitis.' *JHEP Reports* 4, no. 5 (May 2022): 100450. Published online February 18, 2022. https://doi.org/10.1016/j.jhepr.2022.100450. PMCID: PMC9011026. PMID: 35434588.

reducing stress and promoting a sense of calm and relaxation, mindfulness may help modulate the immune system and prevent it from attacking healthy tissues.

Incorporating mindfulness techniques into treatment plans for autoimmune disorders can provide patients with effective strategies for managing their symptoms and maintaining optimal health. It is increasingly evident that embracing mindfulness can greatly improve physical health for those seeking optimal wellness.

Psychological and Emotional Benefits

Delving into ancient mindfulness teachings can also unlock a wealth of benefits for psychological and emotional well-being. Meditation and self-reflection can enhance emotional regulation, increase self-awareness, and foster a sense of inner peace. By tapping into ancient wisdom traditions, individuals can navigate the complexities of modern life with greater resilience and emotional equilibrium.

Mindfulness can significantly decrease the need for external validation and societal pressures in individuals. By focusing on the present moment and cultivating self-awareness, individuals can better understand their values, beliefs, and strengths, which can greatly increase self-confidence. This increased sense of self-awareness allows them to rely less on external sources for validation or approval, making them more resilient in the face of societal pressures.

Mindfulness also helps individuals develop an internal locus of control, empowering them to make decisions based on their values rather than conforming to external expectations.

Strategies for Conquering Challenges in Mindfulness Practice

In today's fast-paced world, characterised by constant stimulation and distractions, integrating ancient mindfulness techniques can truly be transformative. By embracing and acknowledging distractions without judgment, individuals can develop a focused and present mindset.

One of the most significant challenges I have faced is establishing boundaries, both within myself and with others. I have learnt that setting clear limits requires a deep understanding of oneself and the ability to prioritise various aspects of life. I experienced burnout as the demands on my time and energy escalated without clear boundaries.

When I experienced work-related stress injuries, I made the difficult decision to put my career on hold. This coincided with a relocation to a different country, providing me with an opportunity to reassess my priorities. While setting boundaries in a professional setting may be easier, I initially struggled due to a lack of understanding of the work culture in a different country.

Reading stories of women who have successfully set boundaries to achieve their goals is inspiring. However, due to a lack of adequate support systems in the countries where I have lived, I found it difficult to establish boundaries in personal relationships. I often felt constrained by traditional gender roles, but I realised that setting boundaries was essential for maintaining a healthy balance between home and work responsibilities.

It has taken me several years and health issues to realise that we are ultimately on our own. The belief that we will always have family members to support us was shattered when reality hit, and I found myself lacking the assistance or emotional support I had hoped for. It became clear that the only solution was to establish strong boundaries regarding what I could and could not handle. Disrupting long-standing habits and expectations was necessary but challenging.

Despite being fully aware of the benefits of setting boundaries in defining expectations, limits, and responsibilities within relationships, I still struggle with implementing them. I now set boundaries based on my own needs, prioritising self-care above all else. I understand that these boundaries are essential for protecting my well-being. It has been a gradual process to explain to others and myself that these boundaries are not meant to create barriers or distance. I communicate that I cannot manage all tasks at once and am prioritising my responsibilities to ensure that my efficiency is not compromised.

Throughout this journey, I have experienced both the loss and growth of relationships. Those individuals with whom I have set boundaries have shown appreciation for my honesty, leading to deeper connections. Most importantly, I have gained a newfound self-respect by acknowledging that I am not a superwoman. I have accepted that if I cannot give my full attention to a situation, it is better to address it later. This may involve delaying responses to e-mails or calls, focusing on one task at a time, or simply communicating my limitations. Taking these steps has been a significant milestone in my personal growth. With that being said, I make sure to not neglect my responsibilities in addressing urgent family needs or requirements. I have just stepped down from being the on-call member of the family.

I have made significant progress in my growth journey, which I attribute to my decision to stop seeking validation from others for every action I take and to be mindful of my physical and emotional boundaries. While I acknowledge that I am fortunate to have the resources to prioritise self-care, I wish I had possessed the wisdom and courage to do so earlier in life. Through consistent practice, I am training my mind to give precedence to self-care and establish healthy boundaries in all areas of my life.

As you begin your mindfulness journey, you may come across individuals who try to divert you from your path towards heightened awareness. It is important to gently educate them on your values, if necessary, and ensure that you stay true to the path you have set for yourself. Stay focused and committed to your personal growth and well-being.

Building Consistency in Mindfulness Practice

Consistency plays a key role in unlocking the benefits of mindfulness techniques. Establishing a routine may pose challenges initially, but by starting small and gradually increasing the time dedicated to mindfulness activities, individuals can cultivate a sustainable habit. Whether it involves setting aside a few minutes each day for meditation or incorporating mindful moments into daily tasks, consistency serves as the foundation for long-term personal growth and transformation.

One effective strategy that I embraced was creating a detailed schedule or to-do list that outlined tasks and allocated specific time for each activity. Prioritising tasks based on their importance and deadlines ensured that critical tasks were completed promptly. Additionally, setting an alarm to wake up at a consistent time may seem traditional, but it proved beneficial in regulating my body's internal clock, leading to heightened energy levels and improved focus throughout the day. Implementing timers for social media apps on my phone helped me resist distractions such as constantly checking e-mails or social media. This practice significantly reduced mental clutter, enhanced time management skills, and ultimately contributed to maximising my overall happiness quotient.

11
Ancient Techniques to Improve Focus

'The greatest weapon against stress is our ability to choose one thought over another.'

—William James

Meditation practices offer a powerful tool for unifying the mind, body, and spirit and are deeply rooted in traditions like Buddhism, Hinduism, Taoism, and Indigenous spiritual beliefs. The word 'meditation' stems from the Latin term *meditatum*, which means 'to ponder'. Before fully grasping the concept of meditation, the word itself often carries a sense of intrigue. It is commonly perceived as something reserved for the wise and enlightened. This perception can serve as a convenient excuse for individuals to avoid delving into the true meaning of meditation and embracing its benefits.

Incorporating ancient wisdom into our daily lives does not have to be daunting. By taking small, actionable steps, such as setting aside time for daily meditation, practising gratitude, or connecting with nature, we can infuse our routines with the transformative power of mindfulness. Embracing ancient wisdom isn't about perfection, instead, it involves the willingness to explore and embody these teachings in our day-to-day experiences.

In the modern-day world that is often filled with distractions and stressors, these ancient meditation tools can offer solace and a path towards self-discovery and enlightenment. Just like one size does not fit all, those who want to embark on the journey of mindfulness and would like to use meditation to calm their nerves must determine what practice suits them best—embracing one method or a combination of them.

Depending on the situation I have been in, I have found it interesting to explore and embrace various techniques to calm my mind. Calming the chatter requires consistency, discipline, and practice. It does not matter what tool you use as long as you use a tool to help you declutter your thoughts.

Regardless of the specific method employed, the underlying principle of all mindfulness techniques remains consistent—to prevent the mind from succumbing to negative thoughts and to cultivate self-awareness. The benefits of these activities, irrespective of the specific routine, are the same:

a. **Heightened Awareness:** Mindfulness helps you notice and deal with your feelings as they happen so you can handle them better.

b. **Reduced Reactivity:** By practising mindfulness, you can learn to watch your feelings without instantly reacting, which helps you think before you act.

c. **Improved Attention and Focus:** Mindfulness helps you pay attention to what's happening right now, instead of getting caught up in negative feelings or thoughts.

d. **Enhanced Self-Acceptance:** Mindfulness teaches you to be kinder to yourself and accept who you are, which can help you feel better about yourself.

e. **Decreased Stress and Anxiety:** Regular mindfulness can lower your stress and anxiety levels, making it easier to handle tough situations.

f. **Better Emotional Balance:** Mindfulness can help you keep your emotions in check by accepting and dealing with them without getting overwhelmed.
g. **Greater Empathy and Compassion:** Practising mindfulness can make you more understanding and caring towards yourself and others, leading to better relationships.
h. **Neuroplasticity:** Mindfulness can change how your brain works, especially in areas that control emotions like the prefrontal cortex and amygdala.
i. **Improved Mood:** Mindfulness is linked to feeling more positive and happier, which can improve your overall mood.
j. **Enhanced Coping Skills:** Mindfulness offers you tools to handle tough emotions and situations; thus, you're less likely to turn to unhealthy coping methods like avoiding problems or using substances.

Best Meditation Positions

Meditation has been around for centuries with numerous benefits for both physical and mental health. One of the key elements of a successful meditation practice is finding the correct position to sit or lie in. There are several meditation positions that practitioners can choose from, each with its own benefits and challenges.

One of the most common meditation postures is the cross-legged sitting position, also known as the lotus or half-lotus position. In this position, the practitioner sits with their legs crossed and their hands resting on their knees. The cross-legged posture is favoured by many meditators because it helps maintain a straight back and promotes good posture and focus. However, it can be difficult for individuals with tight glutes or knee pain. An alternative position is the kneeling posture, where the practitioner sits on their heels with their knees apart. This position may be more comfortable for those with tight glutes or knee issues, but it could be challenging for individuals with ankle pain.

Another popular meditation posture is the lying down position, where the practitioner lies on their back with their arms resting by their sides. This position is often preferred by those with back pain or discomfort in the hips or knees. However, lying down can make it easier to fall asleep during meditation. It is important to stay alert and focused while in this posture to avoid dozing off. No matter which meditation position a practitioner chooses, it is crucial to find a comfortable and stable position that allows for deep breathing and a clear mind. By experimenting with different positions and finding what works best for them, individuals can enhance their meditation practice and reap the many benefits that come with a regular meditation routine.

Contemplation Meditation Technique

Meditation means 'to ponder'. Whilst all kinds of meditation involve reflecting deeply on a specific concept, idea, or question, there is a specific type of contemplation technique, where the purpose is to think or contemplate on the situation given or a phrase used.

The Koan Technique

The koan technique is a practice used in Zen Buddhism to attain enlightenment through the contemplation of paradoxical statements or questions. The word koan comes from a Chinese term and can be loosely translated to 'precedent' or something that happened in the past. Its goal is to stop overthinking and listen to your gut. Each koan technique teaches one something about Zen and tests how well they understand it.

These koans are typically short phrases or stories that challenge the rational mind and encourage practitioners to move beyond conceptual thinking. By pondering upon these enigmatic riddles, individuals may experience a breakthrough in their understanding of reality and their true self.

One famous Zen koan goes like this: 'When both hands are clapped, a sound is produced; listen to the sound of one hand clapping.' It is akin to a brain teaser, encouraging one to think outside the box. Our minds are conditioned to seek meaning and purpose in everything. However, the koan aims to disrupt this way of thinking. It presents a question without a definitive answer, challenging our usual rationale. The mind struggles to comprehend and accept this lack of meaning, but ultimately, it must acknowledge the question as it is—without inherent meaning or rationale. Just like in life, we must learn to accept certain things and surrender to the uncertainties. The koan technique largely teaches one acceptance.

Compassionate Meditation Techniques

This meditation is rooted in the belief of focusing on the feelings of kindness and empathy to develop a greater sense of connection with others, ultimately alleviating feelings of isolation and loneliness. One of the key components of compassion meditation is sending positive thoughts and intentions towards oneself as well as others. This practice involves generating feelings of warmth and kindness towards oneself, loved ones, acquaintances, and even strangers.

Ho'oponopono Meditation

Ho'oponopono is a traditional Hawaiian practice of reconciliation and forgiveness that has gained popularity recently for its powerful healing effects on individuals and relationships. The Hawaiian word ho'oponopono roughly means 'to make things right'. The practice involves taking full responsibility for one's thoughts, actions, and emotions, and releasing any negative energies causing discord or pain. By acknowledging and apologising for any harm caused, seeking forgiveness from others, and expressing gratitude and love, ho'oponopono helps restore balance and harmony within oneself and with others.

One of the core beliefs of ho'oponopono is that our external reality reflects our internal state. By resolving inner conflicts and releasing negative patterns, we can create positive shifts in our external experiences. This practice emphasises the power of forgiveness, compassion, and love in healing past wounds and repairing relationships, which leads to a deeper sense of peace and well-being. Through ho'oponopono, individuals learn to let go of resentment, anger, and blame, focusing on cultivating acceptance, kindness, and understanding towards themselves and others. Ho'oponopono can be a transformative tool for personal growth, inner peace, and building stronger connections with those around us.

At the heart of ho'oponopono are four powerful phrases: I'm sorry, Please forgive me, Thank you, and I love you. These phrases release negative emotions, heal past traumas, and cultivate a sense of love and gratitude.

One of the tools used in ho'oponopono today is called CEEPORT®, created by Dr Ihaleakala Hew Len and stands for 'Clean, Erase, Erase until you reach the PORT'. The PORT is the Zero State—a state of pure potential. For instance, if I wished to clear blocks relating to opportunities in my life, I would say the prayer:

> I am sorry for not always embracing opportunities that came my way.
>
> Please forgive me if I did not treat those well who showed me the opportunities.

Thank you for the awareness within me that opportunities will open when we seek them.

I love you that everything is happening at its highest good.

CEEPORT
CEEPORT
CEEPORT

Loving-Kindness Meditation

Loving-Kindness Meditation is also known as LM or metta meditation and is based on the ancient Buddhist tradition known as metta-bhavana. The word metta has its origin in Pali. It could also have originated from *Maitri* in Sanskrit, which means friendliness and loving-kindness. The word bhavana means 'the act of'. Through this practice, individuals develop feelings of kindness and compassion towards themselves, their loved ones, and even those they perceive as difficult or challenging. By directing these positive emotions towards others, practitioners can break free from negative thought patterns and develop a sense of interconnectedness with all living beings.

A well-known Sanskrit mantra that you can chant is: 'Lokāḥ Samastāḥ Sukhino Bhavantu [May all beings everywhere be happy and free (of suffering and sadness)].'

Tonglen Meditation

Tonglen meditation is a traditional Tibetan Buddhist practice that involves the deliberate cultivation of compassion by exchanging oneself with others. In this meditation, practitioners focus on breathing in the suffering and negativity of others and exhale positive energy, love, and healing vibes.

This powerful technique helps individuals develop empathy and compassion towards others and assists them in releasing their attachments to self-centred thoughts and emotions. Pema Chödrön, a renowned Buddhist teacher, author, nun, and mother, has shared teachings on the practice of Tonglen, which can be easily accessed on the internet. This technique is simple to learn and doesn't require formal education, making it accessible for those who approach it with sincerity.

Vipassana Meditation

Vipassana meditation, or insight meditation as it is called, originates from ancient Buddhist teachings and focuses on self-observation and self-awareness. Vipassana means 'to see things as they are' and is one of the most ancient meditation techniques. This method emphasises developing insight into the true nature of reality by observing sensations within the body without reacting to them. Practitioners are taught to cultivate mindfulness and equanimity through prolonged periods of silent meditation, typically spanning ten days in a rigorous retreat setting. Those who attend this course must follow the five precepts:

- Abstain from killing any being
- Abstain from stealing
- Abstain from all sexual activity
- Abstain from telling lies
- Abstain from all intoxicants

By developing the capacity to impartially observe physical sensations and emotions, individuals can gain a deeper understanding of themselves and break free from the conditioned patterns of reactivity. This is an intensive course and may not be suitable for everyone. Additionally, it may be a good idea to take care of personal commitments before embarking on such an intensive course.

Whilst I understand that not everyone can become Buddha by practising meditation, I do know that the outcome of this meditation technique is to create your understanding of where you want to be in your life.

Ritualistic Meditation Techniques

Rituals play a crucial role in shaping spiritual journeys and enriching communal life. They provide structure, meaning, and a shared experience, acting as anchors in the turbulent seas of life.

Mindfulness, like sending your mind to the mental gym, focuses on the present moment without judgment. Rituals add intention and meaning to everyday actions, enhancing focus, awareness, and well-being. From lighting a lamp to breaking bread, rituals come in various forms, each unique yet carrying universal themes of devotion, connection, and reverence. This can include creating a specific space for meditation, using props like cushions, lamps, and incense sticks, and incorporating repetitive movements or mantras to guide attention.

Integrating rituals into mindfulness routines involves personalising them to align with individual preferences and needs. Whether it's a morning meditation or an evening gratitude practice, tailoring rituals to suit your style makes them more meaningful and sustainable. Consistency is essential—setting specific times and cues, staying flexible with adjustments, and celebrating small wins help maintain momentum.

Embrace rituals as sacred moments of reflection and intention to tap into deeper self-awareness and present-moment connection. Approach them with an open mind and curiosity, experiment with different practices, and seek support from the community or mentors to cultivate deeper mindfulness in everyday life.

Kolam, Shakyo, and Mandala Art

Shakyo, mandala, and kolam are traditional forms of meditative practices that have been used for centuries in various cultures. These practices not only promote relaxation and inner peace but also aid in developing heightened levels of awareness and spiritual connection by creating or reproducing these sacred symbols.

Shakyo, originating from Japan, involves the meticulous handwritten reproduction of Buddhist sutras to focus the mind and cultivate mindfulness. It was introduced as a religious practice but has now evolved into a form of Zen meditation.

Mandalas, found in Tibetan Buddhism and Hinduism, are intricately designed geometric patterns that symbolise the universe and serve as a tool for concentration and contemplation.

Kolam, a traditional art form from South India, consists of intricate patterns drawn on the ground using rice flour or coloured powders to invite positive energy into the house and enhance mental clarity during meditation. Despite having lived in various countries and experienced different cultures, I have always found it both calming and captivating to create a kolam design at the entrance of our home during festivals. I recall a light-hearted incident that occurred when I drew a kolam in front of our house in Canada. It was a splendid late autumn day, coinciding with a festival of lights, and we were expecting guests for dinner. I carefully drew the beautiful Swastika kolam at the entrance, only to have my husband rush out and insist that I remove it immediately. He was concerned that it bore too close a resemblance to the Nazi swastika, despite my attempts to explain the stark differences. The Nazi symbol, or Hakenkreuz, features a right-angled rotation, and 45-degree angled arms, and lacks the four dots present in the traditional Kolam. I obliged and removed the kolam, replacing it with another intricate design made of rice flour, allowing the visiting ants and birds to feed on it and creating a warm welcome for our guests.

Like the increasingly popular art of doodling, these practices require mental and physical engagement, with elements of yoga postures being incorporated involuntarily to ensure precision in the artwork. Numerous shakyo, kolam, and mandala worksheets are available online that cater to all skill levels, from beginners to advanced. By dedicating time every day to practise drawing Kolam or mandala work, one can gradually master different designs and eventually transition from paper to floor using chalk. This consistent practice improves attention span and provides a sense of accomplishment and tranquillity.

Sound Bath Meditation

Sound bath meditation is a transformative practice that harnesses the power of sound vibrations to guide individuals into a state of deep relaxation and inner harmony. Originating from ancient healing traditions, sound bath meditation has gained popularity in modern wellness practices for its ability to reduce stress, promote mental clarity, and enhance overall well-being.

It involves immersing oneself in the soothing sounds of various instruments, such as crystal singing bowls, tuning forks, gongs, and chimes. This therapeutic technique provides a deeply relaxing experience that helps reduce stress and anxiety, improve sleep quality, and promote overall well-being. During a sound bath session, participants lie down comfortably while the practitioner plays these instruments in a carefully orchestrated manner to create harmonious vibrations that resonate throughout the body. The sound waves produced by these instruments can shift brainwave states into more meditative states, inducing a sense of calmness and tranquillity.

Sound bath meditation can be a powerful addition to your self-care routine. Whether you practise it daily, weekly, or whenever you need a moment of relaxation, incorporating sound baths can help you unwind, recharge, and reconnect with yourself. Experiment with different techniques, instruments, and frequencies to find what resonates best with you and creates a space for deep relaxation and inner peace.

I practise sound bath meditation by ringing the bell in my home's temple/altar/sacred space every morning. I light the lamp first thing in the morning, say my prayers, offer whatever I have to offer for that day to the deity, and ring the bell. This ritual brings a great sense of peace for two reasons. First, it frees my mind of the hallucinated state that we sometimes experience upon waking up, allowing me to get on with my day's work. Second, the chime of the bell reminds me of my childhood memories of my father walking around with a bell and lamp in his hand, appeasing pictures of each deity (over 50 of them) that he had placed on the altar. I feel delighted that I am continuing traditions I now understand better.

Lighting a Lamp

The tradition of lighting a lamp holds deep cultural and spiritual significance across various societies worldwide. This ancient ritual symbolises dispelling darkness and the pursuit of knowledge and enlightenment. Beyond mere illumination, lighting a lamp is a sacred practice that invokes blessings, positivity, and divine energies. The act of igniting a flame carries profound symbolism and is deeply rooted in ceremonies and everyday life, transcending the boundaries of religion and culture. From the serene temples of India to homes in the West, lighting a lamp symbolises hope, knowledge, and light, which resonates universally. This timeless ritual, with origins dating back to ancient times, has evolved to encompass cultural nuances and spiritual beliefs while retaining its essence of illumination and reverence.

In today's fast-paced world, lighting a lamp has gained new meanings. Modern interpretations of this ritual emphasise mindfulness, self-care, and intention setting. Whether through scented candles for relaxation or digital lamps in virtual ceremonies, the symbolism of illuminating light is a potent symbol of hope and positivity. Embracing the daily practice of lighting a lamp can foster grounding and mindfulness, providing a sense of sacredness to ordinary moments—whether at the start of the day or before retiring for the night, kindling a flame can set the tone for the day ahead or facilitate a peaceful transition into rest. Nurturing this ritual can infuse everyday life with mindfulness and sacredness.

Trataka Meditation

Also known as focused gazing, trataka is a traditional yogic practice that involves fixing one's gaze on a single point or object. This technique boosts concentration, mental clarity, and overall focus. By gazing at a candle flame, a black dot on the wall, or any other visual stimulus, practitioners can achieve a calm state of mind and deep concentration. As the mind becomes absorbed in the chosen focal point, distractions and thoughts dissipate, which leads to a heightened sense of awareness and presence. Trataka meditation is particularly advantageous for individuals seeking to improve their mindfulness practices or address emotional blockages.

Chanting Meditation Techniques

Chanting can focus your mind and create a sense of calm and inner peace, making it an excellent technique for developing mindfulness. Repeating rhythmic sounds or phrases helps calm the mind's endless chatter, allowing individuals to focus on the present moment. Chanting makes one deeply aware of their breath and body sensations, grounding them in the present. By regularly chanting, individuals can develop heightened awareness extending beyond the practice, enabling them to cope with life's various challenges with greater clarity, concentration, and emotional stability.

Chanting Mantras

Chanting mantras is a centuries-old practice in Hinduism and Buddhism that involves the repetition of sacred sounds, words, or phrases to develop a spiritual connection or achieve a desired outcome. The rhythmic and melodic nature of chanting helps practitioners focus their minds, creating a meditative state, which further allows them to immerse themselves in the vibrations and energy of the mantra.

In my last book, *Ancient Chants for Modern Living*, I elaborated on the positive effects of chanting on the emotional well-being of a person with fictional stories and appropriate chants.

Zikr Meditation

Zikr meditation, also known as Dhikr meditation, meaning remembrance, is a spiritual practice rooted in Islamic tradition. It involves the repetitive recitation of specific phrases or names of Allah while focusing on their meaning and significance.

Transcendental Meditation

Transcendental meditation (TM) is a technique from India, developed by Maharishi Mahesh Yogi in the 1950s, which involves silently repeating a specific mantra to achieve a state of deep relaxation and heightened awareness. TM is known for its simplicity and accessibility, making it popular among individuals seeking stress relief, improved focus, and spiritual growth.

Movement Meditation Techniques

Movement meditation combines mindfulness and physical movements to help individuals achieve relaxation and mental clarity. This practice is rooted in various traditions like yoga, t'ai chi, and qigong, emphasising the importance of connecting the mind and body through intentional movements.

Zhan Zhuang

Zhan zhuang, also known as standing meditation, is a traditional Chinese practice that involves holding a static standing posture for an extended period. It is commonly used in martial arts, qigong, and traditional Chinese medicine to cultivate internal energy (qi) and improve physical and mental well-being. By grounding the feet, aligning the spine, and relaxing the body while maintaining awareness of breath and posture, individuals can improve their balance, strength, concentration, and overall health.

One might notice the striking similarity between zhan zhuang and tadasana. Tadasana, or mountain pose, is a foundational yoga pose that emphasises stability, strength, and grounding. By embodying the steadfastness of a mountain, practitioners can cultivate a sense of balance and resilience in their daily lives. Similarly, zhan zhuang, a standing meditation practice from the world of Qigong, focuses on developing internal strength, improving posture, and enhancing energy flow. By standing still like a tree, practitioners can connect with their inner power and find stillness amidst the chaos.

Qigong

Qigong, pronounced 'chi gong', is a holistic practice rooted in traditional Chinese medicine that focuses on cultivating and balancing one's life energy or qi. This ancient practice involves gentle movements, meditation, controlled breathing exercises, and visualisation techniques to promote health and vitality. By harmonising the flow of qi through the body's energy channels, known as meridians, practitioners aim to enhance overall physical and mental well-being. Qi gong has been shown to improve posture, flexibility, coordination, immune function, and emotional stability. Qigong can help reduce stress, alleviate chronic pain, boost energy levels, and strengthen the body's natural healing abilities.

T'ai Chi

T'ai chi, also known as t'ai chi ch'uan, is a traditional Chinese martial art that focuses on slow, deliberate movements and meditation. It is often referred to as 'moving meditation' because of its emphasis on mindfulness and awareness of the present moment. T'ai chi is performed for its numerous health benefits, including improved balance, flexibility, strength, and mental well-being. Research has shown that regular practice of t'ai chi can help reduce stress, alleviate anxiety and depression, lower blood pressure, and improve overall cardiovascular health.

Due to the slow and controlled movements of t'ai, it is easily accessible to people of all ages and fitness levels.

Guided Meditation Techniques

Guided meditation is a powerful practice that involves listening to a trained professional or recorded audio guide leading you through a meditation session. By following the instructions, participants can quiet their minds, connect with their breath, and explore their inner world in a safe and supportive environment. Guided meditation often incorporates visualisation exercises, breathing techniques, and body scans to deepen the meditative experience.

According to research, regularly performing guided meditation can have numerous benefits for physical and mental health including lowering blood pressure, improving sleep quality, reducing anxiety and depression symptoms, and increasing feelings of overall well-being. In a study conducted by Burgstahler et al,[4] it was found that daily mindfulness meditation for five to twelve minutes is linked to reduced

4. Matthew S. Burgstahler and Mary C. Stenson, *'Effects of Guided Mindfulness Meditation on Anxiety and Stress in a Pre-Healthcare College Student Population: A Pilot Study'* (2020).

stress and anxiety as well as increased mindfulness with more significant effects shown after longer sessions.

This kind of meditation was first introduced to me by my cousin. While she suggested several guided meditation techniques that worked for her, what finally drew me to this practice were the playlists of Jason Stephenson. Guided meditation can be performed by lying down, in a seated position, or even while walking. The guide's voice helps bring your attention back to the present and your breath. Different guided meditations can be performed in any position as long as you are comfortable.

Body Scan Meditation

Most mindfulness exercises always include a body scan exercise wherein you become aware of every organ in your body. The closest parallel in yoga is shavasana or corpse pose. The yoga teacher brings awareness to each body part—from the soul of your feet to the base of your head. The mind and body significantly relax at the end of this body scan technique.

Continuous practice of this technique helps us reach a non-judgmental state, accepting ourselves first and then accepting those around us.

Keyif Meditation

Keyif is a powerful and transformative practice rooted in the ancient Sufi tradition that focuses on cultivating inner peace, harmony, and spiritual growth. This form of meditation involves connecting with one's breath, engaging in visualisation techniques, and reciting sacred mantras or prayers to calm the mind and access deeper awareness. By combining mindfulness, deep breathing exercises, and guided imagery, keyif meditation helps individuals achieve a heightened sense of presence and self-awareness.

Energy Meditation Techniques

Energy meditation is a powerful technique that involves harnessing and directing the body's energy for healing and self-improvement. This practice is based on the belief that everything in the universe is made of energy, and by tapping into this energy through focused meditation, individuals can improve their physical, emotional, and spiritual well-being.

Energy meditation techniques can vary but usually comprise visualisation and breathwork to attune the body's energy centres or chakras.

Kundalini Meditation

Kundalini meditation technique is a spiritual practice rooted in the ancient Indian tradition of kundalini yoga, where the base of the spine's energy is awakened through powerful sounds or words known as mantras. The term 'kundalini' refers to this latent power located at the base of the spine, like a coiled serpent. Chanting the kundalini mantras, allows the energy to rise through the seven chakras of the body that, when awakened, can result in self-realisation and spiritual enlightenment.

A popular Kundalini mantra is *Sat Nam*, which means 'truth is my identity.' It is stated that by using this mantra, the practitioner can release illusions and false identities by establishing a connection with their higher self and inner truth. Practitioners usually begin with breathwork and chants to activate this energy, followed by specific postures and movements to stimulate its flow.

The four stages of Kundalini practice help elevate one's consciousness, enhance intuition, and cultivate a profound sense of unity with the divine forces that guide and support them on their spiritual journey.

Chakra Meditation

Chakra meditation originates from ancient Indian traditions, based on the belief that the body has seven energy centres, or chakras, along the spine. Each chakra corresponds to different physical and emotional aspects of one's being. Practitioners aim to balance and harmonise their energy levels by focusing on these energy points during meditation. This form of meditation promotes overall well-being and inner peace by enhancing the flow of energy throughout the body.

During chakra meditation, individuals may visualise each chakra as a spinning wheel of energy. It starts from the base of the spine with the root chakra and moves upwards to the crown chakra at the top of the head. By focusing on each chakra individually and working to release any blockages or imbalances, practitioners aim to restore balance and alignment within themselves. This practice may involve deep breathing exercises, visualisations, and affirmations to help cleanse, activate, and harmonise the energy centres. The seven chakras come with their specific colours and mantras along with their functionality that we can focus on to improve ourselves:

1. Muladhara Chakra or Root Chakra is located at the pelvic floor and the base of the spine. It is visualised using the colour red. The function of this chakra is survival, and the mantra used is *Lam*.
2. Svadhisthana Chakra or Sacral Chakra is located three inches below the navel and is visualised using the colour orange. The function of this chakra is desires, and the mantra used is *Vam*.
3. Manipura Chakra or Solar Plexus Chakra is in the navel, below the rib cage, and it is visualised using the colour yellow. The function of this chakra is intellect, and the mantra used is *Ram*.

4. Anahata Chakra or Heart Chakra, located near the centre of the chest, is visualised using the colour green. The function of this chakra is compassion and unconditional love, and the mantra used is *Yam*.
5. Vishuddha Chakra or Throat Chakra is in the throat area and is visualised using the colour blue. The function of this chakra is acceptance, and the mantra used is *Ham*.
6. Ajna Chakra or the Third Eye Chakra is in the middle of the forehead and is visualised using the colour indigo. The function of this chakra is the perception of truth, and the mantra used is *Om*.
7. Sahasrara Chakra or the Crown Chakra is located on top of the head and is visualised using the colour purple or violet. The function of this chakra is freedom from illusion. No specific mantra is used for this chakra as silence is maintained at this point.

Reiki Healing

Reiki, an alternative medicine from Japan, involves transferring universal energy from the practitioner to the patient to promote healing and balance. It is based on the belief that energy flows through all living beings and disruptions can lead to illness. Practitioners aim to remove blockages and restore the body's natural ability to heal itself through gentle touch or by placing their hands near the body. Reiki helps to remove blockages and facilitate the flow of vital energy in the body. This allows for the release of negative emotions and thoughts that can hinder mindfulness practice. By promoting inner balance and harmony, Reiki enables individuals to quiet the mind and fully engage in meditation or mindfulness exercises, leading to a deeper and more enriching experience.

I vividly remember when I had finished my first level of Reiki healing there was a gentle prayer that the healer imparted. She was a Christian by birth and chose to incorporate the Lord's prayer while healing the energy. I still use this prayer when I feel troubled:

Angel of God, my guardian dear,
To whom God's love commits me here,
Ever this day, be at my side,
To light and guard,
Rule and guide.
Amen!

Pranic Healing

Pranic Healing is an alternative form of energy healing that focuses on manipulating and balancing the body's vital energy, known as *prana*. Developed by Grand Master Choa Kok Sui, this practice involves using the hands to scan, cleanse, and manipulate the energy field surrounding the body. It is based on the belief that imbalances in the body's energy field can lead to physical, emotional, and mental ailments. By correcting these imbalances, the body can heal itself more efficiently.

Pranic healing removes energy blockages and imbalances to help achieve deep relaxation and inner peace. This state of well-being allows for greater awareness and presence, making mindfulness practices such as meditation and breathwork easier.

A friend of mine introduced me to the Pranic healing prayer on forgiveness. This affirmation, coined by Master Choa Kok Sui, involves visualising the person who has hurt us in front of us and mentally chanting the prayer below. Afterward, you would cut the imaginary energy cord between you and the individual.

Namaste!
We all are children of the most high.
I salute the Christ in you,
the Buddha in you,
the divinity within you,
Namaste!
God's blessings be with you!
I will not talk to you.
I will not interact with you.
I refuse to be entangled by you!
I will keep my distance from you!
Go in peace!

Seated Meditation Techniques

Ancient civilisations like India, China, and Japan have long embraced seated floor practices to connect with the divine and achieve mental clarity. These practices have transcended generations and borders, becoming an integral part of various belief systems. Seated floor practices offer myriad benefits that encompass physical, mental, and spiritual well-being, making them a holistic approach to self-care and personal growth. These practices include sitting on the ground in a cross-legged position, focusing on the breath or an object in the front.

Seated meditation can be performed anywhere in a safe place as long as there are no external distractions. Wear loose clothing and sit on an erect chair or the floor in any sitting asana (mentioned in chapter 12). Allow your body to choose the position that it finds comfortable. In sitting meditation, simply allow the body and mind to calm the chatter and allow yourself to focus on your breathing. It can be challenging to control your thoughts as they arise but embrace them and bring your focus back to your breath.

Mudra Meditation

Mudra meditation is a unique and powerful technique that uses hand gestures or positions to channel energy and enhance focus. The Sanskrit word 'mudra' means 'seal' or 'gesture', and in the context of meditation, mudras symbolise certain states of consciousness or qualities. By incorporating mudras into meditation, practitioners can deepen their connection to their inner selves and experience a greater sense of unity and tranquillity.

One of the crucial aspects of mudra meditation is the understanding that each finger and hand position corresponds to different elements and energies within the body. By manipulating the fingers and hands into specific mudras, individuals can stimulate and balance these energies, leading to a more harmonious state of being. For instance, the Gyan mudra, which involves touching the tip of the index finger to the tip of the thumb, is believed to promote wisdom, knowledge, and clarity of thought. Incorporating this mudra into meditation can help practitioners access a profound level of understanding and insight by focusing on the sensations and positions of the hands to release distractions. This physical component of mudra meditation can be particularly useful for individuals who struggle to calm the inner chatter or maintain their focus during meditation sessions.

Zazen Meditation

Zazen meditation, often referred to as seated meditation, is a fundamental practice in Zen Buddhism that focuses on developing mindfulness and presence through the simple act of sitting. Performed primarily in a quiet and still environment, zazen involves assuming a specific posture with a straight back, hands forming a mudra, and eyes partially open to maintain alertness. The practitioner then focuses on their breath, observing thoughts as they arise without judgment or attachment.

Visualisation Meditation Techniques

Visual mediation techniques help calm the mind by taking you on a virtual tour of nature using visualisation. Just as the mantras of the deities allowed us to visualise ourselves based on their strengths, such as positive qualities, these visualisation techniques help us harness strength from the object of the visualisation.

Henosis Meditation

Henosis meditation is a powerful spiritual practice that stems from ancient Greek philosophy and mysticism. Henosis is derived from the Greek word for 'oneness' or 'union', and it focuses on achieving unity with the universe and the divine through intense concentration and visualisation techniques. Here, practitioners typically enter a state of deep contemplation, often focusing on symbolic images, sacred sounds, or mantras to facilitate the process of spiritual awakening.

Kemetic Meditation

Kemetic meditation is a spiritual practice rooted in ancient Egyptian beliefs and customs. It involves deep introspection, visualisation, and the use of sacred symbols to connect with the divine energies of the universe. The use of ancient Egyptian symbols, such as the ankh (symbol of life), the Eye of Horus (symbol of protection and healing), and the Djed pillar (symbol of stability), is common. These symbols are focused upon during meditation to tap into the wisdom and power of these gods and goddesses to guide them on their spiritual journey.

In ancient civilisations, symbols were more than just drawings, they were powerful tools that conveyed ideas, beliefs, and emotions. From religious expressions to cultural identity, symbols were integrated into various aspects of society. Ancient civilisations like Mesopotamia, Egypt, Greece, and Rome utilised symbols extensively for communication, religious rituals, and artistic expressions. Egyptian hieroglyphs were not just pretty pictures but a sophisticated writing system that combined phonetic and symbolic elements. They adorned temples, tombs, and scrolls, conveying tales of pharaohs, gods, and the afterlife. In a world buzzing with symbols, ancient ones still hold a special kind of wisdom. We can tap into a timeless source of guidance, inspiration, and connection to our collective past by understanding their power, embracing their meanings, and incorporating them into our modern lives.

Central to Kemetic meditation is the principle of Ma'at, emphasising the importance of living in alignment with truth, justice, and balance. Kemetic meditation offers a unique and profound experience for individuals seeking personal growth, transformation, and spiritual connection in a way that honours the ancient traditions of Egypt.

Mountain Meditation

Since time immemorial, mountains have been integral to the stories of ancient civilisations. In many societies, mountains were considered the habitats for the gods and goddesses as well as locations for sacred rituals and ceremonies. Mountains greatly defined the narratives of ancient myths by serving as settings for epic stories about bravery, conquests, and adventures. In Greek mythology, twelve Olympians resided at the top of Mount Olympus and ruled over earthlings. Similarly, in Hinduism, the Himalayas are regarded as a holy mountain range, home to several gods and sages.

Mountains were often identified with mightiness, power, and eternity. The towering heights and roughness of mountains symbolised the unimaginable strength and authority these deities possessed over nature. In other mythologies, climbing a mountain often indicated spiritual realisation or overcoming human weaknesses. Sometimes, the dangerous journey to its summit was an assessment of one's courage and resilience. The challenging landscape and severe weather conditions of the mountains represented the hero's tests and difficulties along with his victory over adversity and rise to greatness. Consequently, mountains functioned as potent symbols of change and individual development in the legends of ancient times.

The purpose of mountain meditation is to become as strong and stable as a mountain and find the ability to stay strong and immovable during times of stress and challenges. It helps develop a sense of inner stability and resilience while promoting deep relaxation and mental calmness.

Sit in a comfortable, upright position, with your feet flat on the ground. Close your eyes and centre yourself, picturing a majestic mountain. Then, visualise yourself as the mountain.

Lake Meditation

Lake meditation is a calming mindfulness practice that uses the image of a lake to promote inner peace, clarity, and tranquillity. Lakes have played a significant role in shaping the course of human history, particularly in ancient civilisations where their presence held immense importance. From serving as vital water sources for sustenance and irrigation to being spiritual and cultural hubs, lakes were integral to the fabric of society. Ancient texts and literature used lakes as symbols of purity, renewal, and transformation, weaving metaphors and allegories that conveyed deeper meanings about life, nature, and the human experience. Understanding the deep connection that ancient societies shared with lakes sheds light on how these water bodies continue to influence and enrich modern society to this day.

Water also plays a crucial role in meditation practices, serving as a metaphor for the ebb and flow of life and the continuous cycle of renewal. Across cultures, water symbolises emotions, intuition, and the subconscious mind. By incorporating water symbolism into meditation, individuals can explore their inner depths and navigate the currents of their thoughts and feelings.

The purpose of this meditation is to notice that, like the lake, you can experience different ebbs and flows of life on the surface, understand the vast expanse of a reservoir of emotions within, and accept that these emotions and phases of life will pass.

Nature-Driven Techniques

We were once gifted a beautiful orchid plant that bloomed magnificently for house-warming. However, our joy was short-lived as the flowers soon withered and the stalks began to dry up. Feeling a sense of sadness, I was unsure of how to properly care for this delicate plant. After visiting a plant nursery and watching instructional videos on YouTube, I learnt that the roots needed to be cleaned and re-potted for the plant to survive. After a few weeks of dedicated care and root restoration, new leaves began to emerge, marking a period of meditative reflection as I nurtured the plant back to health.

Similarly, the Tulsi plant, revered in India for its numerous benefits like increasing positive vibrations and oxygen levels in homes, requires delicate care. In Hindu households, Tulsi plants are grown and tended to with great reverence, as it is considered inauspicious for a Tulsi plant to wither or die. This belief instils a sense of focus and dedication in caring for the plant. Individuals may experience a heightened awareness and connection with nature, engaging all five senses. This holistic approach to health and wellness highlights the importance of slowing down and appreciating the natural world around us.

Shinrin-Yoku

Shinrin-yoku or forest bathing is an ancient Japanese practice that underscores the deep relationship between human beings and the natural world. It has been used through various cultures in history because of its therapeutic and rejuvenating effects. Many cultures considered nature sacred, and forests were highly respected as places where individuals could receive healing, enlightenment, or connect with divinity.

In the distant past, forest bathing was part of ceremonies and rites were carried out during significant events in life. These rituals helped people deepen their spiritual connections and nurture a sense of belonging to the natural world. Groves and other natural landscapes were considered sources of spiritual healing by ancient cultures. They also used these natural spaces for practices like meditation, herbalism, and energy work, all aimed at promoting holistic well-being.

As a therapeutic practice shinrin-yoku has gained widespread recognition for its ability to reduce stress, reduce blood pressure, and boost immune system function. Research has shown that spending time in natural environments can have a calming effect on the nervous system, leading to decreased cortisol levels and improved mood. Many health professionals recommend shinrin-yoku as a preventative measure against burnout and mental fatigue in this fast-paced society.

The modern resurgence of forest bathing has sparked a renewed interest in nature-based therapies and holistic wellness practices. As more people seek refuge in natural spaces to escape the stresses of urban life, forest bathing has gained popularity as a restorative and rejuvenating activity.

The 5-4-3-2-1 Grounding Technique

This technique involves focusing on sensory experiences like touch, smell, taste, sight, and sound to anchor oneself in the present moment and alleviate feelings of anxiety or distress. The 5-4-3-2-1 grounding technique is a mindfulness exercise designed to bring individuals back to the present moment and reduce feelings of overwhelm, anxiety, or dissociation. It involves systematically engaging all five senses by noting five things you can see, four things you can touch, three things you can hear, two things you can smell, and one thing you can taste. By focusing on these sensory experiences, individuals can anchor themselves in the present moment and detach from intrusive or distressing thoughts.

This technique is commonly used in therapeutic settings to help clients regulate their emotions and cope with intense feelings. In my family, I applied this technique to the elderly people. Most seniors appear to be filled with deep regrets during their golden years. While unfortunate, I found this approach highly effective in bringing them back to the present. I asked them to consider the 5-4-3-2-1 method, and they did remarkably well until they reached the point where they had to identify one thing they could taste. The elders in our household struggled with creativity as it had been a while since their last meal—all they could come up with was 'saliva'. Is there really a taste to saliva? Take a moment and try tasting your saliva—the versatility of this liquid might surprise you.

The Pachamama Technique

The concept of Mother Earth is ubiquitous and has its roots in prehistoric belief systems. It has great cultural and civilisational significance. Honoured as a nourishing and vital energy source, Mother Earth represents how all living things are interdependent with the environment. Ancient societies revered the earth as a sacred being that embodied attributes of wisdom, abundance, and healing through rituals, symbolism, and mythology, representing the cyclical nature of life, regeneration, and abundance. Ancient customs placed a strong emphasis on the spiritual bond that exists between Earth and humanity. It was thought that this link provided direction, healing, and a feeling of acceptance in the natural world.

The goal of Pachamama meditation—a spiritual discipline with roots in Andean Indigenous traditions—is to establish a connection with Mother Earth. Symbolic objects like sacred stones, vibrant fabrics, and coca leaves are frequently used in Pachamama rites. Offerings are made to Pachamama as tokens of appreciation and reciprocity, such as food, flowers, and incense. Shamans play a role in ceremonies for healing and reestablishing harmony between the natural world and humanity. Through chanting, rituals, and spiritual interventions, shamans invoke Pachamama's healing energy and guidance.

Practitioners believe that by meditating on nature and honouring the Earth as a living being humans can deepen their connection to the natural world and nurture feelings of gratitude, harmony, and balance. This type of meditation often requires individuals to visualise themselves blending with the natural elements and drawing upon their healing qualities.

The age-old custom of paying respect to Pachamama has found a new home in vibrant cityscapes. With the help of rituals, sacrifices, and meditations, urbanites gather in parks, on roofs, and in community centres to reestablish their connection with the planet. Though the Andean mountains may appear far away from the urban jungle, Pachamama's spirit lives on in these contemporary adaptations.

Friluftsliv Technique

Friluftsliv, a Norwegian term that translates to 'open-air living', is a concept that highlights the importance of connecting with nature and spending time outdoors every single day even if it is snowing.

Rooted in Norway's cultural and historical relationship with the natural world, friluftsliv promotes physical health, mental well-being, and environmental stewardship. It also encourages individuals to seek out experiences in the wilderness through hiking, camping, or simply spending time in green spaces.

Walking

Babies usually start walking when they are 10–18 months old. They walk cautiously, taking every step with utmost caution—perhaps a good lesson for those who jaywalk on the road! Walking is shown to help boost mood and increase blood circulation in the body. A brisk walk every day not only helps in mental but also in the improvement of memory processes.

Walking is also known to positively influence the hypothalamic-pituitary-adrenal axis—the Central Nervous System—responsible for the stress response. The amygdala is a group of brain cells responsible for strong emotions such as anger and fear. The amygdala is responsible for correlating the memory and the emotion that transpired when associated with that memory. In his book, *Hardwiring Happiness*, author Rick Hanson talks of how a bad experience sticks onto the memory much easier than a good experience. One can assume that is why it is harder for people with a prolonged state of stress to find it challenging to be happy, as their memory of happy times is replaced by stressful times.

Mindful walking for at least 30 minutes every day can significantly reduce stress. Embrace the following techniques that have helped me personally:

1. Create a playlist of songs or podcasts you want to listen to before you embark on the walk to avoid being distracted. Use earplugs and keep your phone in your pocket.
2. Wear comfortable clothes and shoes.
3. Be more aware of the places you are walking by—the surroundings, sights, and sounds.

4. Set a timer or alert in terms of destination or the completion of the playlist, so you don't have to keep looking at your phone or watch to know when to head back home.
5. Set a goal for the number of steps you want to walk that day to feel accomplished after completing the goal. Make sure to keep a pace that suits you and your fitness level. Remember, it is not a race.

Challenges in Meditation

Mindfulness practice is intentionally being aware of one's thoughts, sensations, emotions, and surroundings without judgment. Forcing the mind to focus on the breath or any other form of meditation can be challenging.

One of the easiest ways to help the mindfulness practice is to focus on just one sense—hearing. My husband and I were on a road trip with our friends and were trying to make it to a wedding in time. I was one of six drivers—including the back-seat drivers! With much to talk about, the car soon became stuffy and noisy for my comfort. I suddenly felt overwhelmed and desperately wanted some fresh air and quiet.

I leaned my head against the window and closed my eyes, desperately trying to shut out the noise around me and analysing the different sounds I heard. There was the rustle of wedding clothes, music blaring from the radio, another friend's voice singing along to her own music, the driver trying to determine under muffled gasps how terrible the roads were, the friend seated on the passenger side reacting with exclamatory noises to the incoming traffic, another friend talking loudly on the phone to the person at the wedding to hold the seat for us, and amidst all that noise was the gentle comfort of my new saree wrapped around me that helped me relax.

When you allow yourself to focus your mind on one sense

without any judgment, you also allow yourself to analyse your reaction and that of your body to all those sounds. That analysis helps you provide the basis and leads you towards meditation—the ability to focus on one sense, analyse the input and your reaction, and process how your body and mind accept all those sounds from that one sense.

Thus, when I closed my eyes and focused on the sounds, they all merged into a single, continuous noise, creating a din in my ears rather than several distinct, disturbing noises. I vaguely remember telling my friends to meditate before I fell asleep and woke up at the wedding destination feeling refreshed and ready to greet the bride and groom.

12
The Power of Breath in Stress Management

'Inhale the future. Exhale the past.'
—Eckhart Tolle

The breath serves as a powerful anchor to the present moment. Utilising breathing techniques for mindful living is an important tool in mindfulness as it enables individuals to enhance their presence and awareness of thoughts, emotions, and physical sensations. Integrating breathing techniques into daily life can result in a heightened sense of calmness and resilience in the face of challenges, leading to improved well-being and quality of life. The upcoming chapters will delve deeper into some of the breathing techniques I follow.

The significance of breath is often overlooked as it is an involuntary process. However, it is undeniable that breath is the most vital aspect of our existence. Jennifer Thorley, an editor and writer, highlighted in her article 'Breath of Life', published in *The Lancet*, that an average human takes approximately 7.5 million breaths per year, totalling around 600 million breaths in a lifetime.

A recent experience at the dentist's office shed light on the profound impact of breathing techniques. During a root canal treatment, a dear friend experienced intense pain despite the administration of a pain-numbing solution. Using simple breathing exercises, my friend's stress levels were regulated, allowing the dentist to successfully complete the procedure without interruption.

Research indicates that altering our breathing patterns and directing our attention to our breath can activate the vagus nerve[5], the longest cranial nerve that extends from the base of the skull to the abdomen. The vagus nerve plays a crucial role in regulating various aspects of the body's fight-or-flight responses, including heart rate, blood pressure, perspiration, and digestion. By stimulating the vagus nerve, individuals can effectively mitigate the effects of the body's stress responses and promote a sense of calmness and mental clarity.

Following breathing techniques can help alleviate stress.

The Physiological Sigh

While listening to a podcast by Andrew Huberman—professor of Neurobiology and Ophthalmology at the Stanford School of Medicine of the Huberman lab—he outlined several techniques to overcome stress and anxiety. One of the techniques that his lab and several other labs are working on is called the 'physiological sigh'. It is a spontaneous response that occurs naturally in the body when we cry, try to fall asleep, experience a build-up of CO2 in the system, or find ourselves in a claustrophobic environment such as a small elevator. This type of sigh can also be considered a coping mechanism of the body in response to stress.

This technique will slow the heart rate, expand the lungs, and calm the mind, gaining control of our emotions.

5. Roderik J. S. Gerritsen and Guido P. H. Band, 'Breath of Life: The Respiratory Vagal Stimulation Model of Contemplative Activity,' *Frontiers in Human Neuroscience* 12 (2018): 397, published online October 9, 2018, https://doi.org/10.3389/fnhum.2018.00397.

a. Take two rapid inhales—even if the second inhale is swift—through the nose. Even if you feel congested, breathe in through your mouth with pursed lips.
b. Follow this up with a long, extended exhale through the mouth.
c. Repeat this 10–12 times.
d. Breathe in and out normally after the repetitions.

Note: If you feel dizzy or uncomfortable after the repetitions, please rest.

Piko Piko

The Hawaiian breathing technique, known as 'ha' or piko piko is based on the concept that energy flows where the mind is focused. Piko is essentially the centre of anything in Hawaiian. For instance, the crown (upper piko) and navel (lower piko) act as two centres for humans. Thus, piko piko essentially means centre to centre. This technique involves slow, intentional breaths coordinated with hand movements to create a calming and meditative experience.

a. Sit in a comfortable position or stand with your legs slightly apart.
b. Close your eyes or focus on an object in front of you and take a few breaths before starting the piko piko breathing.
c. Inhale from your navel for two counts and visualise filling up your crown with your breath.
d. Exhale with the sound 'ha' while reaching your arms above your head towards the cosmos. Thank the universe for all that you have and for the energy it provides.
e. Inhale the unlimited supply of energy back from the cosmos.

f. Exhale with the sound 'ha' and bring your arms down slowly as you visualise the energy travelling through your body into the navel.

As we progress through the breathing exercises, remember to focus on the crown of your head during inhalation and your abdomen during exhalation. Thoughts, feelings, and images may arise—acknowledge them and let them pass as we continue for ten breaths:

> Inhale. Haaaaaa. Inhale. Haaaaaa. Inhale. Haaaaaa. Inhale. Haaaaaa. Inhale. Haaaaaa. Inhale. Haaaaaa. Inhale. Haaaaaa. Inhale. Haaaaaa. Inhale. Haaaaaa. Inhale. Haaaaaa.

Diaphragmatic Breathing

The diaphragm is a thin, dome-shaped muscle that sits between the lungs and the heart and helps in the respiration process. During inhalation, the diaphragm contracts and flattens, causing the chest cavity to expand. This action creates a vacuum, drawing air into the lungs. Upon exhalation, the diaphragm relaxes and returns to its dome-like shape, expelling air from the lungs.

My yoga teacher recommends performing this breathing technique in a supine position. This breathing exercise can help you relax and reduce stress. Practise it regularly to improve your breathing technique and promote a sense of calm:

a. Lie on your back on a flat surface or in bed with your knees bent.
b. Place one hand on your upper chest and the other on your belly, just below your rib cage.
c. Take a slow, deep breath in through your nose, allowing the air to fill your lower belly. Keep the hand on your chest still while the hand on your belly rises.

d. As you exhale through pursed lips, tighten your abdominal muscles and allow them to fall inwards, towards the mat, so that you can feel the small of your back on the mat. The hand on your belly should move back down to its original position.

Smriti or Sati Meditation

Anapanasmriti or Anapanasati meditation, also known as mindfulness of breathing, is a traditional meditation technique rooted in ancient yogic practices. *Anapana* means 'inhalation and exhalation' and *sati* means 'awareness'. During Anapanasati meditation, the practitioner does not exercise any control over the breath (as in Pranayama) but simply observes their breath.

Here, the practitioner focuses on the natural rhythm of their breath, observing its flow without trying to control or manipulate it. By paying close attention to the sensations and movements associated with breathing, individuals develop heightened awareness and concentration.

a. To begin practising Anapanasati meditation, sit upright in a comfortable cross-legged position. Close your eyes and focus on your breath; pay attention to each inhale and exhale.
b. As you breathe, count your breaths in cycles of ten. Inhale (one), exhale (two), and continue until you reach ten. Once you have counted to ten, repeat the cycle.
c. Throughout your practice, be mindful of any negative thoughts or feelings that may arise. Instead of holding on to them, allow them to pass by like clouds in the sky. Observe your thoughts without judgment.

By following these steps, you can cultivate a sense of calm and clarity in your mind. Practise regularly to experience the full benefits of Anapanasati meditation.

Daoist Breathing

Daoist breath technique, also known as Daoist breathing or Daoist breathwork, is a fundamental aspect of Daoist practices that aims to cultivate vital energy and promote inner harmony. This ancient Chinese tradition focuses on the regulation of inhaling and exhaling to balance Qi, or life force energy, throughout the body. It involves deep inhalation through the nose, filling the abdomen with air, followed by a slow exhalation through the mouth, completely emptying the lungs.

The most common type of Daoist breathing practice is reverse breathing. It is aptly named due to its stark contrast with natural breathing patterns.

a. Begin by taking a deep breath in.
b. Contract your abdomen, filling the upper portion of your lungs.
c. Exhale and push your abdomen out, allowing the breath to drop within your body. This process results in decreased pressure within the lungs, causing the diaphragm to move downwards, contracting the organs in the abdomen.

This technique is used in strength training as a strong core provides increased power and stability, making it advantageous to exhale while contracting the muscles.

Yogic Breathing Technique

Several asanas or breathing exercises in yoga greatly help to reduce stress. Outlined below are some techniques known to bring down stress levels considerably.

Yogic breathing is used in most pranayama. The main requirement is that respiration be comfortable and relaxed, with the breath flowing naturally and not being forced.

a. Sit in a meditative posture or lie in shavasana and relax the whole body.
b. Inhale slowly and deeply and place your right hand on your abdomen to expand fully.
c. Try to breathe softly so that little to no sound of the breath can be heard. Feel the air reaching into the bottom of your lungs.
d. At the end of the abdominal expansion, expand your chest outward and upward.
e. When the ribs fully expand, inhale some more until the expansion is felt in the upper portion of the lungs around the base of your neck. Your shoulders and collarbone should also move up slightly. You will feel some tension in the neck muscles.
f. The rest of the body should be relaxed.
g. Feel the air filling the upper lobes of the lungs. This completes one inhalation.
h. The entire process should be one continuous movement, each phase of breathing merging into the next without any obvious transition point. There should be no jerks or unnecessary strain; the breaths should be like the swell of the sea.
i. Now exhale.
j. First relax the lower neck and upper chest, then allow it to contract downward and then inward.
k. Allow the diaphragm to push upward and towards the chest.
l. Without straining, try to empty the lungs as much as possible, drawing or pulling the abdominal wall as close to the spine as possible. The movement should be harmonious and flowing.

This completes one round of yogic breathing. Initially, perform 5–10 rounds and slowly increase it to 10 minutes daily.

Anuloma Vilom

Anuloma vilom is an alternate nostril breathing technique, which helps with a wide variety of problems including alleviating stress and insomnia, increasing lung capacity, and minimising allergic conditions such as a blocked nose and hay fever.

In anuloma vilom, the air is inhaled from the left nostril and exhaled from the right; then the inhalation is done in reverse.

a. Sit in sukhasana and close your eyes.
b. Place your right hand in Vishnu mudra by folding the index and middle fingers inward.
c. Close your right nostril with your thumb and breathe out completely through your left nostril.
d. Now breathe in through your left nostril for as long as you can comfortably.
e. Close your left nostril with your ring and little fingers, and exhale through your right nostril for as long as you can.
f. Now inhale again through your right nostril, close it, and exhale through your left.

This completes one round. Repeat at least 10–15 times and try to make your breath long and smooth.

Sama Vritti Pranayama

Box breathing, or Sama Vritti pranayama, is a type of pranayama that focuses on taking slow breaths. United States Navy Seals practise this technique to regulate their emotions during stress. It can also be used to calm one's thoughts and release repressed emotions.

a. Exhale fully to a count of four.
b. Hold your lungs empty for a count of four.
c. Inhale to a count of four.
d. Hold the air in your lungs for a count of four before exhaling.
e. Repeat the same process as many times as desired.

Ujjayi Pranayama

Ujjayi breathing helps stimulate the vagus nerve, leading to a sense of calmness and altering the mental state. It has several other benefits like balancing the thyroid hormones by activating the thyroid gland. It is also known as a tranquilising pranayama.

a. Sit in a comfortable position, preferably in a meditation asana.
b. Close your eyes and relax your entire body.
c. Focus on the breath flowing through your nostrils, allowing it to become calm and rhythmic.
d. After a few moments, shift your awareness to the throat area.
e. Try to feel or imagine that the breath is entering and leaving through the throat rather than the nostrils as if inhalation and exhalation are occurring through a small throat aperture.
f. As your breath naturally slows and deepens, gently contract the glottis to produce a soft snoring-like sound, like the breathing of a sleeping baby. This should lead to a simultaneous contraction of the abdomen, happening effortlessly.
g. Ensure both inhalation and exhalation are long, deep, and controlled.

h. Continue practising yogic breathing while focusing on the sound created by the breath in the throat.
i. The sound should be audible to you but not loud enough for others nearby to hear unless they are very close.
j. Once you have mastered this breathing technique, curl the tip of your tongue back into the mouth until it touches the soft palate just below the nasal cavity (khechari mudra).
k. If your tongue becomes tired, release it briefly while maintaining the Ujjayi breathing. Resume folding the tongue back when rested.
l. Practice this technique for 10–20 minutes.

Pranakarshan Pranayama

Pranakarshan pranayam was developed by Pandit Shri Ram Sharma Acharya. This pranayama is a combination of deep conscious breathing and meditation on the vital force, which is present in the universe in the form of light and energy.

'Prana principle full of light and energy pervades it. Prana akin to clouds of hot steam shining in sun light are flowing towards us from all directions. And within this Prana we are seated contentedly, peacefully and joyfully.

a. Sit cross legged and place both hands on the knees and close your eyes.
b. Inhale through both nostrils, focusing on the idea that we are drawing in clouds of the Prana principle into the body. Prana enters through the nose and spreads to other organs.
c. After inhaling deeply, hold the breath without exhaling and mentally affirm: 'The Prana I have breathed in is now permeating every pore of my body.' Just as Mother

Earth absorbs every drop of rain that falls, every breath, too, is being absorbed into our entire body.

d. Hold the breath comfortably without exhaling for a moment, then exhale slowly while thinking: 'Having absorbed the essence of Prana into every pore of my body, impure air is being expelled.'

e. After exhaling completely, retain the breath outside for a while, experiencing a moment without air, and reflect: 'Having exhaled all impurities of my mind, I will shut all doors on them. These distortions have now fled far from me.'

f. Repeat this cycle at least five times.

The 4-7-8 Breathing Technique

This breathing technique is based on several principles of pranayama and was developed by Dr Andrew Weil. This is known to help with insomnia, increase the oxygen supply in the body, and calm the mind extensively.

a. Breathe out completely through your mouth, making a whooshing sound.

b. Close your mouth and inhale through your nose to the count of 4.

c. Hold your breath for a count of 7.

d. Breathe out of your mouth for a count of 8, making a whooshing sound.

e. Repeat these steps as much as desired.

Addressing Common Meditation Challenges

The word meditation comes from the Latin word *meditatum*, which means to 'concentrate' or 'to ponder'. Practising meditation (in the right way) has several benefits, and it needs no elaboration.

Meditation can be tough because it's challenging to quiet your mind and focus. Many individuals struggle with controlling their thoughts and feelings, which makes it tricky to relax and concentrate. It's also not easy to find a quiet place and time to meditate in our busy lives. Distractions, like noises or your own thoughts, can come in the way of your meditation practice and make you feel frustrated. Plus, if you're new to meditation, you might feel uncomfortable trying out different techniques and poses. To get better at meditation, you must be patient and practise regularly. Being mindful and self-aware can help you deal with these challenges and feel more peaceful and balanced when you meditate.

My venture into meditation started with guided meditation. I found it extremely difficult to get to sleep and anxious thoughts crowded my mind. These thoughts affected not just my sleep but also my daily routine the next day. I found listening to someone telling me to focus on things, other than what was crowding my mind, helped me tremendously.

The guided meditation was very effective, and it helped me to sleep better. However, I faced another issue soon—I could not extend my meditation practice beyond a point. I started feeling sleepier earlier. To counteract this drowsiness during meditation, I tried changing my posture and sat upright on a pillow.

Practising Bhramhari or Bhastrika pranayama a few times helped in waking me up from my drowsiness during meditation. Engaging in deep breathing exercises can help increase oxygen flow to the brain, keeping the mind awake and focused. It is also helpful to meditate when you are naturally more awake and alert, such as in the morning or after engaging in physical activity. Avoiding heavy meals or caffeine intake before meditation can further support staying awake and attentive during practice.

Own your meditation practice. Every person's comfort in practising meditation is individualised and what works for one may not work for another. Find ways that work for you.

13

Asanas to Enhance Meditation

'Yoga is not about touching your toes. It is what you learn on the way down.'

—Jigar Gor

Tittham caram nisinno vā
sayāno vā yāvat' assa vigatamiddho,
etam satim adhittheyya
brahmam Etam vihāram idha-m-āhu.

Standing, walking, sitting
or lying down, as far as possible without sluggishness
this mindfulness should be undertaken
[It is like] dwelling with God here and now.

The above paragraph—and its translation—is an excerpt from the Metta Sutta. Metta meaning loving kindness and Sutta meaning the discourse of Buddha, talks about the rules of meditation. According to the scriptures, meditation can be performed in any position—standing, walking, sitting or lying down—as long as you are comfortable and can remain calm and alert. Standing postures are particularly beneficial for preparing the body for meditation as they help improve posture, overall strength, and flexibility. These postures also strengthen the muscles used to maintain a straight and relaxed back during meditation. On the other hand, seated and lying meditation postures may be more suitable for beginners.

Posture is crucial during meditation for several reasons:

a. **Promotes Alertness**: A proper posture helps keep you awake and attentive. Sitting with a straight spine prevents you from becoming too relaxed and falling asleep.
b. **Enhances Breath Flow**: An upright posture allows for better lung expansion, promoting deeper and more efficient breathing, essential for relaxation and focus.
c. **Reduces Discomfort and Pain**: Proper alignment minimises physical strain on your body, reducing the likelihood of discomfort or pain that can distract you from your meditation practice.
d. **Encourages Mental Clarity**: Good posture supports a clear and focused mind. When your body is aligned, it can prevent mental sluggishness and maintain alertness.
e. **Facilitates Energy Flow**: Many meditation traditions believe that an upright posture aids in the free flow of energy (prana) throughout the body, enhancing overall effectiveness.
f. **Symbolises Intent**: Sitting with a dignified posture can symbolise your intention and commitment to your meditation practice, reinforcing a sense of purpose and discipline.

Regardless of the yoga pose, make sure to address the following aspects of the body.

Spine and Shoulders

By focusing on proper shoulder and spine postures, you can enhance your meditation practice, reducing physical discomfort and maintaining better focus. When meditating, it's essential to sit up or stand straight to stay focused and in control. Imagine your spine to be a stack of coins, lined up perfectly. Proper shoulder posture during meditation is essential for comfort and effectiveness. Here are key points to consider:

a. **Relaxed Shoulders**: Keep your shoulders relaxed and not hunched. Let them fall naturally, away from your ears, to reduce tension.
b. **Aligned with Spine**: Ensure your shoulders are not slouched or pulled back too tightly.
c. **Symmetry**: Avoid having one shoulder higher than the other. Both shoulders should be at the same level.
d. **Open Chest**: An open chest promotes better breathing. Gently pull your shoulders back to open your chest; however, avoid overextending.
e. **Support with Cushion**: If sitting cross-legged on the floor, use a cushion to raise your hips. This can help align your spine and shoulders more comfortably.
f. **Arm Position**: Rest your hands on your knees or your lap. Doing this keeps your shoulders relaxed and stable.
g. **Mindful Adjustments**: Periodically check your shoulder posture during meditation. Make small adjustments to maintain comfort and alignment.

Chin Posture

The position of your chin during meditation is important for maintaining proper alignment and ensuring a comfortable and effective practice. Your head and neck should be in line with your spine as well. Don't tense your muscles or stiffen up. Sit straight and focus on your breathing.

Here are some guidelines for optimal chin posture:

a. **Slightly Tucked**: Keep your chin slightly tucked towards your chest, as it elongates the back of your neck and aligns your spine.
b. **Neutral Position**: Avoid lifting your chin too high or dropping it too low. The goal is to maintain a neutral position where your head feels balanced on your spine.

c. **Gaze**: Whether your eyes are open or closed, let your gaze be soft and directed downwards at a gentle angle. If your eyes are open, you can focus on a spot a few feet in front of you on the ground.
d. **Avoid Tension**: Ensure that your chin position does not create tension in your neck or shoulders. The tuck should be gentle and natural.
e. **Alignment Check**: Periodically check your alignment during meditation. Your ears should be over your shoulders, and your chin should follow this natural alignment.

Hand Postures

The position of your hands during meditation can significantly affect your comfort and focus. Any hand position works as long as you don't feel the weight of your spine, shoulders, neck, or head on your hands. Here are several common and effective hand postures to consider:

1. **Resting on Knees**:
    - Palms Down: Place your hands on your knees with palms facing down. This can help ground and calm you.
    - Palms Up: Place your hands on your knees with palms facing up. This can help you feel more open and receptive.
2. **On Your Lap**:
    - Dhyana Mudra: Rest your hands on your lap, palms up, with the right hand on top of the left hand, with the thumbs gently touching, forming a circle. This is common in Zen and Buddhist meditations.
    - Cupped Hands: Rest your hands on your lap, cupped

together with fingers overlapping, and thumbs touching lightly.

- Gyan Mudra: Touch the tip of your thumb to the tip of your index finger, forming a circle. Extend the remaining three fingers straight. Place your hands on your knees with palms facing up. This mudra is believed to enhance concentration and wisdom.
- Chin Mudra: Touch the tip of your thumb to the tip of your index finger, forming a circle. Extend the remaining three fingers. Place your hands on your knees with palms facing down. This mudra is believed to instil spiritual enlightenment and wisdom—commonly used with breathing techniques like Anuloma Vilom, Nadi Shodhana, and Ujjayi Pranayama.

3. **Relaxed and Natural**: Let your hands rest comfortably wherever they naturally fall, such as on your thighs or lap. This is particularly useful for beginners or those seeking a less formal posture.
4. **Hand Positions with Beads**: If you use *mala* or prayer beads, hold them with your thumb and middle finger, and let the beads rest on your lap or knee.

Standing Positions for Meditation

Several standing asanas can be used for meditation, combining the benefits of physical stability and mental focus. Standing poses for asanas might sound counterintuitive to meditation but are used where practitioners find it difficult to sit or lie down to meditate. This type of meditation is helpful if you tend to feel drowsy while practising seated meditation. Below are a few standing asanas that are well-suited for meditation.

Tadasana (Mountain Pose)

Stand with your feet together or hip-width apart. Distribute your weight evenly across both feet. Engage your thighs and lift your kneecaps. Lengthen your spine and keep your shoulders relaxed. Your arms can hang by your sides or be placed in a prayer position at your chest.

Benefits: Improves posture, balance, and body awareness. Provides a solid foundation for meditation.

Vrksasana (Tree Pose)

Stand on one leg and place the sole of the other foot on your inner thigh or calf, avoiding the knee. Bring your hands to prayer position at your chest or raise them overhead. Focus on a point in front of you to maintain balance.

Benefits: Enhances balance and concentration. Promotes grounding and stability.

Garudasana (Eagle Pose)

Stand with your knees slightly bent. Wrap one leg over the other, and, if possible, hook your foot behind your calf. Extend your arms in front of you and wrap one arm over the other, bringing your palms together. Hold the pose and breathe deeply.

Benefits: Improves focus, balance, and flexibility. Enhances concentration and awareness.

Virabhadrasana I (Warrior I Pose)

Stand with your feet hip-width apart. Step one foot back and turn it out slightly. Bend your front knee, keeping it over your ankle. Raise your arms overhead, palms facing each other. Keep your hips squared to the front.

Benefits: Builds strength and stamina. Opens the hips and chest, promoting deep breathing.

Virabhadrasana II (Warrior II Pose)

Start in Tadasana and then step your feet wide apart. Turn your right foot out and your left foot slightly in. Bend your right knee over your ankle. Extend your arms parallel to the floor and gaze over your right hand. Keep your torso upright.

Benefits: Enhances stability, focus, and endurance. Opens the chest and improves circulation.

Uttanasana (Standing Forward Bend)

Stand with your feet hip-width apart. Hinge at your hips and fold forward, allowing your upper body to hang down. Keep a slight bend in your knees if necessary. Let your hands rest on the floor, your shins, or hold opposite elbows.

Benefits: Calms the mind, stretches the hamstrings and back, and relieves stress.

Utkatasana (Chair Pose)

From Tadasana, step your feet hip-width apart. Inhale and bend the knees as if sitting on an imaginary chair. Lower the hips while keeping your weight in your heels. Extend your arms straight overhead, parallel to each other with palms facing inward or keep them shoulder-width apart. Lengthen your spine, engage your core and stay in the pose for several breaths.

Benefits: Strengthens the mind, boosts blood circulation, enhances balance, and develops core strength.

Padahastasana (Hand to Foot Pose)

Begin in Tadasana, standing tall with your feet together and arms at your sides. Inhale deeply, raising your arms overhead to elongate your spine. Exhale and hinge at your hips, folding forward. Keep your spine long as you move, leading with your chest. Place your hands under your feet, with your palms facing upward and your toes touching your wrists. Allow your head and neck to hang freely, releasing any tension. Your gaze should be towards your legs or shins. Keep a slight bend in your knees if necessary, especially if you have tight hamstrings. Over time, work towards straightening your legs as flexibility improves. Take deep, steady breaths while in the pose, allowing your body to relax further with each exhale. Maintain the pose for several breaths, focusing on lengthening your spine and deepening the stretch with each exhale. To come out of the pose, release your hands, engage your core, and slowly roll up to standing, one vertebra at a time. Finish in Tadasana.

Benefits: Padahastasana provides a deep stretch to the hamstrings, calves, and Achilles tendons. The compression of the abdomen during the forward fold stimulates the digestive organs, improving digestion. The forward bend promotes relaxation and can help to reduce stress and anxiety, providing a calming effect on the mind.

Parsvottanasana (Pyramid Pose)

Begin in Tadasana, standing tall with your feet together and arms at your sides. Step your left foot back about 3–4 feet, keeping your hips facing forward. Your left foot should be angled out slightly, about 45 degrees. Ensure your hips are squared to the front of your mat. You may need to adjust the width of your stance to achieve this alignment. Inhale deeply, lifting your arms overhead to lengthen your spine. Exhale and hinge at your hips, folding forward over your right leg. Keep your spine long and your torso reaching forward as you move. Place your hands on the floor beside your right foot—on your shin or yoga blocks if you cannot reach the floor comfortably.

Press firmly into both feet, engaging your quadriceps and keeping your legs strong and active. Allow your head and neck to hang freely, releasing any tension. Your gaze should be towards your right shin or knee. Take deep, steady breaths while in the pose, focusing on lengthening your spine and deepening the stretch with each exhale. Maintain the pose for several breaths, feeling the stretch in your hamstrings, calves, and hips.

To come out of the pose, inhale and slowly rise, leading with your chest. Step your left foot forward to meet your right foot and return to Tadasana. Step your right foot back and repeat the pose on the opposite side.

Benefits: Stretches the hamstrings and calves, opens the hips, improves balance and stability, calms the mind, and enhances digestion.

Seated Positions for Meditation

Seated positions are commonly used for meditation because they provide stability and comfort, essential for prolonged practice. Below are several seated positions for meditation along with tips for achieving proper alignment.

Sukhasana (Easy Pose)

Sit cross-legged with your feet resting comfortably on the floor. Keep your spine straight, shoulders relaxed, and hands resting on your knees or lap.

Benefits: Provides a simple and comfortable position for beginners, promoting relaxation and ease.

Padmasana (Lotus Pose)

Sit cross-legged, with each foot placed on the opposite thigh. Your spine should be straight, and your hands can rest on your knees or lap.

Benefits: Creates a stable base, enhances concentration, and promotes deeper meditation. Not suitable for everyone due to flexibility requirements.

Ardha Padmasana (Half Lotus Pose)

It is similar to the Lotus Pose but with one foot placed on the opposite thigh and the other foot tucked under the opposite knee.

Benefits: Provides many benefits of the Lotus Pose with less strain, making it more accessible.

Vajrasana (Thunderbolt Pose)

Kneel on the floor with your knees together and your feet slightly wider than your hips. Sit back so your hips rest on the floor, on your feet. You can place a cushion or block under your hips for comfort.

Benefits: Stretches the thighs and ankles, provides a stable base, and promotes an upright posture.

Virasana (Hero Pose)

Similar to Vajrasana, kneel on the floor with your knees together and your feet slightly wider than your hips. Sit back so your hips rest on the floor between your feet. Place a cushion or block under your hips for comfort.

Benefits: Stretches the thighs and ankles, provides a stable base, and promotes an upright posture.

Seiza (Japanese Sitting Pose)

It is similar to the Hero Pose but with your hips resting on a cushion or bench placed between your feet.

Benefits: Reduces strain on the knees and ankles, allows for a straight spine, and provides a formal sitting posture.

Siddhasana (Accomplished Pose)

Sit with one heel pressed against the perineum and the other one placed in front of the first heel. Your knees should be on the ground, and your hands can rest on your knees or lap.

Benefits: Provides a stable base, promotes spinal alignment, and enhances energy flow.

Burmese Posture

Sit with your legs crossed, but instead of stacking your feet on your thighs, place both feet on the floor in front of you. The legs are not stacked, and the position is less strenuous than Lotus or Half Lotus.

Benefits: Easier on the knees and ankles, suitable for longer meditation sessions, promoting stability.

Chair Sitting

Sit on a chair with your feet flat on the floor, knees at a 90-degree angle, and your back straight without leaning against the backrest. Place your hands on your thighs or lap.

Benefits: Accessible for those with mobility issues or :difficulty sitting on the floor. Provides stability and comfort for longer sessions.

Finding the right seating position for meditation depends on your body's flexibility and comfort. Experiment with different positions and use props like cushions, blocks, or benches to support your practice and maintain proper alignment.

Lying Down Positions for Meditation

Lying down poses for meditation can be particularly useful for those who find sitting uncomfortable or need extra support. Here are some common lying down poses, along with their descriptions and benefits.

Savasana (Corpse Pose)

Lie flat on your back with your legs extended and slightly apart. Allow your arms to rest at your sides with palms facing upwards. Close your eyes and relax your entire body, focusing on your breath.

Benefits: Promotes deep relaxation, reduces stress, and allows for a meditative state of rest. It helps integrate the benefits of meditation or yoga and calms the mind.

Supta Baddha Konasana (Reclining Bound Angle Pose)

Lie on your back and bring the soles of your feet together, allowing your knees to fall out to the sides. Place cushions or blocks under your knees for support, if needed. Your arms can rest at your sides or on your abdomen.

Benefits: Opens the hips and groin, promotes relaxation, and supports deep breathing. This pose can be calming and restorative, aiding in mental and emotional release.

Supta Matsyendrasana (Supine Reclining Twist)

Lie on your back with your knees bent and feet flat on the floor. Gently lower your knees to one side while turning your head in the opposite direction. Extend your arms out to the sides or place them on your abdomen.

Benefits: Stretches the spine and lower back, improves spinal mobility, and aids digestion. The gentle twist also helps to calm the nervous system.

Matsyasana (Supported Fish Pose)

Lie on your back with a bolster or rolled-up blanket placed under your shoulder blades, allowing your head and neck to rest comfortably on the floor. Extend your legs and place your arms at your sides with palms facing up.

Benefits: Opens the chest and shoulders, stimulates the heart, and promotes deep relaxation. It can also aid in relieving tension in the upper body and improve breathing.

Viparita Karani (Legs-up-the-Wall Pose)

Sit next to a wall and lie back, extending your legs up the wall while keeping your hips close to it. Rest your arms at your sides or on your abdomen. Use a folded blanket under your hips if needed.

Benefits: Improves circulation, reduces swelling in the legs, calms the nervous system, and relieves lower back tension.

The benefits of practising mindfulness and gratitude in yoga extend beyond our time on the mat. By applying what we learn during practice to our daily lives, we can face challenges with grace, remain present in each moment, and cultivate gratitude for everything we have.

In yoga, we can focus on each movement and breath. This helps synchronise our body, breath, and mind smoothly and mindfully. By paying attention to how each pose feels and how we breathe, we can deepen our practice and attain a sense of calm and clarity. Aligning our bodies in yoga poses goes beyond preventing injuries and building strength; it is also a practice of mindfulness. Being aware of our alignment allows us to tune into our bodily sensations, thoughts, and emotions, enhancing our self-awareness and presence during practice. Practising yoga with self-compassion means treating ourselves with kindness, which promotes a healthier relationship with ourselves. By accepting ourselves and avoiding self-judgment, we learn to extend kindness and understanding to ourselves even when not on the mat.

Remember, mindfulness and gratitude are ongoing practices, not achievements to be attained and forgotten.

14
Mastering Time Management for Mindful Living

'The trouble is, you think you have time.'
—Buddha

Multitasking has long been viewed as a badge of honour, particularly for women. However, it is important to redefine multitasking as 'performing many tasks, but not simultaneously.' It is crucial to add a disclaimer that performing tasks simultaneously can lead to injury and can be detrimental to physical and mental health. Caution is advised when attempting to multitask.

Various strategies can help individuals become more mindful of allocating their time to different tasks to achieve productivity. Multitasking lies on the opposite end of the spectrum of mindfulness. Embracing mindfulness becomes much easier when we learn to effectively manage our time.

To improve time management, we must pay close attention to our tasks and be mindful of our needs. The proverbial chicken or egg situation—are we more mindful because we manage our time better, or do we manage our time better because we are more mindful? The solution to this complex yet simple issue is unique to each individual and requires practice. Time management techniques and tools establish discipline and focus on completing tasks without distractions like social media or phones.

Mastering time management empowers individuals to take control of their schedules and reduce feelings of overwhelm. This disciplined approach enables individuals to effectively prioritise tasks and transform time into valuable assets. The techniques outlined below are self-regulated and require dedication to cultivate discipline, awareness of personal limitations and strengths, and an understanding of available resources. As individuals hone their time management skills, they are better prepared to embark on the journey of mindfulness.

These techniques also serve as tools to assist you in optimising your time. It is ultimately up to you to adapt these techniques to meet your needs and requirements. Engaging in mindful activities such as cooking, eating, and focusing on tasks that demand full concentration can be practised without succumbing to the temptation of multitasking by using the time management methods outlined below.

Disclaimer: I have utilised several techniques that have proven effective in helping me manage my time more efficiently. At the time, I was unaware of incorporating a blend of the methods mentioned below. However, while researching for this book, I discovered the scientific principles behind time management. This realisation validated my approach, and I was pleased to see how well it aligned with my and my family's needs.

Cultural Influences on Time

Cultural influences play a significant role in shaping our perception and understanding of time. Different cultures have unique concepts of time, which can impact everything from daily routines to long-term planning. For instance, when we lived in the West in places like Canada and the U.K., I found that those cultures prioritised punctuality and efficiency, viewing time as a limited resource that must be carefully managed. In contrast, many Eastern cultures, such as India or Southeast Asia, have a more cyclical view of time; they consider it interconnected with nature and the rhythm of life. This, I noticed, led to a more relaxed attitude towards schedules and deadlines.

Cultural beliefs and values play a significant role in shaping the pace at which events unfold, impacting the interactions and activities within societies. Some cultures may embrace a faster or slower tempo in their daily lives. For example, individuals in India or Thailand may engage in leisurely conversations for extended periods without a specific agenda, while in the West, individuals often feel compelled to fill every minute of their day with activities, possibly influenced by a lack of domestic assistance.

Having experienced various cultures, I have found myself constantly adapting to the varied time management practices that each culture adheres to. As a result, there are instances where my sense of urgency may be perceived as unnecessary by individuals in cultures that were not used to it. This dynamic often influenced my responses to situations, leading to potential conflicts between differing perspectives and ideas.

Time Blocking

Time blocking is a strategic method that involves dividing your day into specific time blocks and assigning tasks to each block. By creating a schedule or planner that outlines all your daily activities, appointments, and tasks, you can effectively manage your time and increase productivity. This approach is similar to how you would plan meetings in a professional setting.

I have recently implemented time blocking to prioritise my exercise and cooking routines, which are essential to my daily schedule. I have observed that many individuals engage in activities such as talking on the phone or watching television while cooking, which, in my opinion, detracts from the enjoyment of these tasks. The only form of multitasking that I engage in is listening to my playlist of songs while walking or exercising, as it helps me stay focused.

It is important to note that time blocking should be flexible to accommodate unexpected emergencies that may arise within the family. By incorporating this method into your daily routine, you can effectively manage your time and achieve a better work-life balance.

The Pomodoro Technique

Developed by Francesco Cirillo in the late 1980s, the Pomodoro technique is a time management method designed to help students break up large tasks and study in 25-minute intervals. This method involves using a timer shaped like a tomato, hence the name 'pomodoro'. Cirillo believed this method to be the most effective way to study.

According to the official website, 'It is a structured method made up of processes, tools, principles and values to learn how to deal with time and turn it from a vicious predator to an ally to boost productivity. It is based on a series of principles built on self-observation and awareness.'

I found myself unknowingly adopting this technique in my writing process. I often become so engrossed in my work that I forget to take breaks and stay hydrated. This led to a realisation that I needed to drink more water. Now, I keep a glass of water next to me while writing and ensure I take breaks every half an hour to drink water and stretch. This routine guarantees I remain hydrated and maintain my physical well-being while working.

The Eisenhower Matrix

Dwight D. Eisenhower, 34th President of the United States of America, was a distinguished general during World War II. Faced with the challenge of making critical decisions daily, he developed the renowned Eisenhower principle.

The Eisenhower Matrix, also known as the Urgent-Important Matrix, assists in decision-making and task prioritisation by categorising tasks based on their urgency and importance. This process helps to identify less urgent and important chores that should be delegated or removed. By prioritising tasks according to urgency and importance, the matrix divides them into four quadrants, each with distinct work strategies.

The Eisenhower Matrix is a powerful tool that helps individuals avoid distractions and establish clear boundaries to meet goals. In France, bankers referred to every financial endeavour as a 'project', emphasising the importance of treating each goal as a separate task that required careful allocation of resources. By viewing each goal as a distinct project and ranking them accordingly, individuals can focus on the most critical tasks while relegating less important ones to the background.

During a conversation with my counsellor, I was feeling overwhelmed by the multitude of tasks demanding my attention. She advised me to identify the four main tasks occupying my time and prioritise them based on their importance. By temporarily setting aside less urgent tasks, I was able to focus my attention on the most critical ones, effectively managing my workload.

Utilising the Eisenhower Matrix, I prioritise my tasks as follows:

1. Do First: Address important tasks that require immediate attention, such as urgent emotional, financial, or health needs of my family members or myself.
2. Schedule: Allocate time for important tasks that are not urgent but still essential. This could be administrative tasks or cleaning.
3. Delegate: Assign tasks that are urgent but less important to others to prioritise effectively. This could be tasks like tending to an overgrown garden or cleaning the roof.

4. Don't Do: Avoid tasks that are neither urgent nor important, as they do not contribute to overall productivity or success. I would add conversations that deplete us of emotional energy and offer no benefit to our personal growth or the relationship itself to this list.

Effective time management is crucial for maintaining a consistent mindfulness practice. Here are some strategies to help integrate mindfulness into a busy schedule. By implementing these strategies, you can better manage your time and maintain a regular mindfulness practice despite a busy schedule.

Time management is essential for creating structure and discipline in your daily life. Here are several strategies to help you achieve this:

1. **Set Clear Goals:** Identify what you want to accomplish each day. Break down larger goals into smaller, manageable tasks.
2. **Prioritise Tasks:** Use the Eisenhower Matrix to categorise tasks by urgency and importance. Focus on high-priority tasks first.
3. **Create a Schedule:** Develop a daily schedule or to-do list. Allocate specific time blocks for each task, including breaks and leisure activities.
4. **Use a Planner or Digital Tools:** Utilise planners, calendars, or time management apps to keep track of your schedule and deadlines.
5. **Establish Routines:** Develop morning and evening routines to start and end your day with structure. Consistent routines can enhance productivity and reduce stress.
6. **Set Time Limits:** Assign specific time limits to tasks to

prevent them from taking longer than necessary. Use Pomodoro Technique to stay focused and take regular breaks.

7. **Eliminate Distractions:** Identify and minimise distractions in your environment. This could include turning off notifications, creating a dedicated workspace, or setting boundaries with others.
8. **Batch Similar Tasks:** Group similar tasks together to improve efficiency. For instance, answer all e-mails in one sitting instead of throughout the day.
9. **Practise Mindfulness:** Incorporate mindfulness to stay focused and present. Mindful practices can help you manage stress and improve concentration.
    - Mindful Moments: Practise mindfulness in short bursts throughout the day. Take a few minutes to focus on your breath, observe your surroundings, or engage in mindful listening during conversations.
    - Combine Activities: Integrate mindfulness with other activities. Practise mindful walking, eating, or even while doing household chores.
10. **Review and Adjust:** Regularly review your schedule and progress. Adjust your plans as needed to ensure you're staying on track and meeting your goals.
11. **Delegate When Possible:** Delegate tasks that others can handle, allowing you to focus on higher-priority items.
12. **Take Care of Yourself:** Ensure you allocate time for self-care, including adequate sleep, exercise, and leisure activities. A balanced lifestyle supports productivity and well-being.

Implementing these strategies can help you create a disciplined and structured approach to managing your time, leading to increased productivity and a more balanced life.

15

Cultivating Clarity and Calm Amid Life's Chaos

'It's all about finding the calm in the chaos.'

—Donna Karan

Amid our busy lives, it is all too easy to get caught up in a never-ending cycle of thoughts, emotions, and distractions that can lead to stress, anxiety, and dissatisfaction.

A series of unfortunate events several years back that began with a call about a job loss, followed by an unwanted conversation with a family member and then ending in an accident, made me wish I had handled things differently. It made me realise the importance of mindfulness in our daily lives. When we practise mindfulness, we can stay calm, focused, and clear-headed, which helps us navigate difficult situations with purpose and intention, ultimately influencing the outcome.

I have always been raised to be a strong woman, following in the footsteps of my ancestors. However, I now realise that everyone has their own timeline for processing challenges. What is a manageable challenge in one setting can become overwhelming in another. It is crucial to give ourselves the time to fully process our emotions. I have learnt the importance of prioritising the processing of emotions over other obligations.

Mindfulness has helped me become more aware and accepting of my emotions. I now view fear, anxiety, and insecurities not as negative emotions, but as signals that I need to address and work through. These emotions are a call for healing and self-care.

Incorporating mindfulness into our routines, whether during meals, conversations, or tasks, can profoundly impact our well-being. Mindfulness is a powerful tool that can help us bridge the gap between our thoughts and actions, leading to a more fulfilling and connected life. Research has shown that regular practice of mindfulness can reduce symptoms of anxiety and depression, improve concentration and cognitive function, and enhance overall well-being.

By focusing on the present moment, we can develop greater self-awareness and emotional regulation, allowing us to respond more effectively to stress and challenges. Integrating mindfulness into our daily activities can improve our quality of life and help us build resilience in the face of life's ups and downs.

Tips to Overcome Overthinking

During the pandemic, between 2021–2022, my father passed away and one of my dogs died, I realised that I needed assistance in navigating my cluttered thoughts. My weakened mental state hindered my ability to organise my thoughts and activities, making it difficult to remain present—a crucial aspect of mindfulness. The overwhelming thoughts of my fragmented family and the challenges I was encountering at that time weighed heavily on me.

Seeking help from a counsellor proved to be a turning point for me. Through simple yet effective methods, she helped me break down my feelings of overwhelm. She began by having me identify the areas that were causing me distress and categorise them into different groups. She then guided me towards prioritising these tasks based on their level of urgency.

After establishing a sense of order, she encouraged me to further dissect these tasks into smaller, manageable pieces. Within these smaller tasks, she prompted me to set specific goals.

Positive Reframing

I have come to realise that overthinking has not led me anywhere productive. However, I have learnt to recognise its presence and implement practical strategies to stop this habit consciously. Whenever my mind becomes overwhelmed with negative emotions, I make a conscious effort to embrace those thoughts. I allow myself to explore them up to a certain point, then question if there is a different approach to solving the issue. If there is, I take the necessary steps to address it. If not, I visualise myself setting it aside for the time being. This method has helped me regain a sense of control and focus on one task at a time, resulting in a more organised and productive mindset.

Habits form in our minds quickly, and it is challenging to get rid of them, especially the negative ones. Nowadays, when I think about resolving a situation, I constantly ask myself if I am able to 'dream like an optimist and plan like a pessimist'. When you plan like a pessimist, you're preparing for the worst-case scenario. This means thinking about everything that could go wrong and creating a backup plan. It may sound negative, but it's a smart way to approach things because it helps you be more prepared for any challenges that may come your way. In the corporate world, this is called proactive risk management. On the other hand, dreaming like an optimist means envisioning the best possible outcome. It's about setting big goals and believing that you can achieve them. This positive mindset can help motivate you to work hard and stay focused on your dreams.

Adopting and embracing this dual mindset is challenging as I constantly need to be aware of how much I allow my emotions to influence my thinking, positively or negatively. I hope that over time this practice will become second nature to me.

Journalling My Thoughts

I believe in the power of writing as a means of self-discovery and self-expression, and it has become a vital part of my journey towards self-awareness and personal growth. I can connect with my emotions, thoughts, and beliefs on a deeper level through the written word. The act of putting thoughts into words allows us to truly understand our innermost feelings and beliefs, helping us to analyse our thoughts more effectively and uncover the reasons behind our emotions.

Over the years, writing has been instrumental in helping me understand my true self, my values, and what I stand for. It is a tool to navigate through confusion and anger, cultivating gratitude. It has also allowed me to reflect on the impact of my actions on future generations.

Practising Gratitude

In the second grade, we were taught the Lord's Prayer. It went like this:

> Thank you, God, for the food we eat,
> Thank you, God, for the world so sweet,
> Thank you, God, for the birds that sing,
> Thank you, God, for everything.

Little did I know then that the valuable lessons on sustainability, environmental consciousness, minimalism, and consumerism were embedded within this prayer. In addition to the spiritual connection it offered, the emphasis on gratitude for even the smallest aspect of life is truly noteworthy.

Only those who suffer from asthma can truly comprehend the profound impact of being able to take a full breath. Thus, whenever I encounter a challenge, I am reminded to look around me and see others facing even greater obstacles. This prompts me to question whether the anxiety I experience stems from past trauma, generational influences, or simply unregulated emotional responses to stressors. Regardless of the cause, I now recognise the feeling of being overwhelmed, but I am also grateful to the universe for revealing solutions to these challenges. By acknowledging that there is always a solution, I firmly believe that not every problem is worth dwelling on. This thought has helped me move on from that state of overwhelm.

Goal-Oriented Activities

To achieve success and productivity in our daily lives, it is imperative to engage in goal-oriented planning of our activities. Setting specific, measurable, achievable, relevant, and time-bound goals enables us to prioritise our tasks and focus our efforts on what truly matters.

Even seemingly mundane tasks such as cooking, cleaning, walking, or waste management can become more engaging and help us stay present when we attach a goal to them. Engaging in goal-oriented activities requires us to measure and monitor our progress, making necessary adjustments to our action plans to ensure goal attainment. This process of reflection and adaptation allows us to stay on course and maintain momentum towards achieving our long-term objectives.

Goal-oriented daily activities foster a sense of purpose and direction in our lives. By aligning our daily tasks with our overarching goals, we can experience fulfilment and satisfaction in our accomplishments. This approach to time management enhances productivity and contributes to one's overall well-being and success in both professional and personal spheres. By proactively planning our daily activities with clear goals in mind, we can unlock our full potential and strive for excellence in all endeavours.

Incorporating goals into daily activities empowers individuals to regain control over their lives and establish a foundation for long-term mental health and well-being.

By taking a few moments each day to focus on the present moment and observe their thoughts and feelings, individuals can cultivate a sense of inner peace and clarity. Mindfulness practices like meditation or deep breathing exercises can help reduce stress levels, enhance concentration, and improve emotional regulation.

Mindfulness exercises mentioned towards the end of the book will help you in your day-to-day life.

16

Mindfulness beyond the Moment: Sustainable Practices for Daily Life

'Wherever you are, be there totally.'

—Eckhart Tolle

The goal of this book is for the readers to be able to be able to incorporate mindfulness into daily routines and habits in a way that is environmentally, socially, and ethically responsible.

Incorporating mindfulness into our daily routines establishes and strengthens our connection with ourselves and our surroundings while promoting a more harmonious relationship with the world around us. This involves being in the moment, performing daily chores required for living, and being mindful of one's impact on the planet—such as reducing waste, conserving resources, and supporting sustainable practices.

When we start practising mindfulness in our daily routines, we will find that we slow down our pace automatically and are not under pressure to keep pace with others' journeys. When we slow down, we become increasingly aware of our limitations and where we need to draw healthy boundaries to respect ourselves and others, too. Our increased awareness benefits our interactions with others—promoting a sense of compassion and empathy towards ourselves and our fellow beings—that transcends fleeting moments. Mindfulness practised in such a manner slowly becomes second nature and more sustainable in daily routines. It benefits individuals on a personal level and contributes to building a more sustainable future for generations.

Creating a Sustainable Mindfulness Routine

The true power of mindfulness is revealed when you incorporate it into your daily routine. Whether you are enjoying your morning coffee or tackling a never-ending to-do list, mindfulness serves as a reliable companion in navigating life's ups and downs. One effective strategy for integrating mindfulness into daily life is to focus on the present moment. This can be achieved through deep breathing exercises, observing one's surroundings, and tuning into the senses. Your breath is your best friend when it comes to mindfulness. Deep breathing can help you relax, reduce stress, and improve your overall well-being. Embrace the power of your breath and make it a priority in your daily routine.

Transform your daily tasks into mindful experiences—washing dishes or walking your dog. Take the time to observe the sights, sounds, and sensations that surround you. When engaging in conversations, give them your full attention. When cooking, focus on the task at hand and appreciate the process. Taking care of your body and skin should be done mindfully, as it directly impacts your health. While eating, avoid distractions such as TV or phones. Even when disposing of garbage, consider the environmental impact of your actions. The key is to be fully aware in every moment, in whatever you do, including the most involuntary actions like breathing.

Another effective method for incorporating mindfulness into daily activities is to schedule specific times for mindfulness practice throughout the day. This could involve morning meditation, short mindfulness exercises during breaks, or integrating mindfulness into routine tasks like eating or driving. You can either start your day with a few moments of gratitude or end it with a peaceful bedtime ritual. Find what works for you and commit to making mindfulness a non-negotiable part of your day.

Mindful Communication

A key strategy for enhancing communication skills is mindful communication. This approach involves being fully present, actively listening to others, and communicating with intention and awareness.

Effective communication is crucial for establishing strong relationships, fostering understanding, and encouraging collaboration. By engaging in mindful communication, individuals can improve their ability to connect with others on a deeper level, prevent misunderstandings, and manage conflicts more effectively.

Reflecting on past experiences, I often wonder if breakdowns in family communication could have been avoided. Were there things left unsaid? Could I have handled situations differently? After much introspection, I have realised that sometimes events unfold in a way beyond our control. This acceptance of destiny is a part of life.

Mindful communication does not require us to constantly play the role of mediator or problem-solver. It simply involves being aware of our emotions and having the courage to acknowledge when a conversation turns too challenging to continue. Often, it can even be just possessing the strength to say, 'I'm sorry, I don't think I am equipped to handle this conversation anymore now. I would appreciate it if we could pick this up later.'

Mindful Observation

When returning to our homeland or revisiting countries we have previously lived in, I am consistently amazed by my ability to navigate these places effortlessly. It wasn't until much later, while delving into the literature on mindfulness, that I realised I had been unknowingly practising mindful observation all along. However, I also recognised that my focus on mindful observation had been limited to external environments, rather than turning inward to explore my own thoughts and emotions. This realisation prompted me to embark on a more profound exploration of mindfulness.

Mindful observation serves as a fundamental practice in fostering awareness and presence in our daily lives. By consciously directing our attention towards our thoughts, feelings, and surroundings, we gain a deeper understanding of ourselves and our interactions with the world. This practice enables us to remain rooted in the present moment, rather than being consumed by past regrets or future anxieties.

I now make a deliberate effort to engage in mindful observation, beginning with active listening and hushing the internal chatter of my mind. I take the time to observe my emotions honestly, acknowledging any distressing situations that arise and seeking ways to cope effectively. Similarly, I recognise moments of joy and try to enhance my happiness through similar experiences.

In essence, the key to success lies in adopting a slow-and-steady approach to mindfulness practice. By cultivating a mindful awareness of our inner and outer worlds, we can navigate life with greater clarity and purpose.

Mindful Cooking

Ayurveda, originating from the Atharvaveda, contains references to the treatment of various diseases using food and plants. Cooking promotes the consumption of healthier meals and enhances awareness of our environment and the ingredients we use.

The art of cooking extends beyond simply preparing food to satisfy hunger. It involves selecting the right ingredients and managing waste effectively. Each step in the cooking process demands attention, skill, and genuine care for those who will enjoy the meal, whether it be yourself or others.

Practising mindfulness requires different focal points for various daily activities. In the realm of cooking, mindfulness is cultivated through attentiveness to each stage of the culinary process. Even if cooking does not come naturally to you, I urge you to spend time in the kitchen to gain insight into the effort and dedication involved in meal preparation.

Cooking is one of the most unique mindful practices that engages all five senses—sight, smell, taste, touch, and hearing. I hold immense respect for individuals facing sensory challenges who excel in the culinary arts. Their ability to cook mindfully, despite limitations, is truly commendable and serves as a testament to the power of embracing mindfulness in all aspects of life.

Mindful Waste Disposal

According to the World Bank, the world generated an estimated 2.24 billion tons of solid waste in 2020, equating to a footprint of 0.79 kilograms per person each day. With rapid population growth and urbanisation, annual waste generation is projected to increase by 73 per cent from 2020 to 3.88 billion tons in 2050.

Each day, we all play a role in contributing to this staggering amount of waste. Recognising this reality and cultivating a desire to protect the planet we call home marked a pivotal moment in my journey towards mindfulness. This involves separating recyclable materials from general waste, reducing overall waste production, and ensuring that hazardous substances are disposed of safely.

Proper management of food waste is a crucial component of sustainable living and environmental preservation. By adopting mindful practices for handling food scraps, we can significantly minimise the volume of organic waste deposited in landfills where it generates harmful greenhouse gases like methane.

Composting is a highly effective technique for disposing of food waste, as it facilitates the natural decomposition of organic matter and enhances soil fertility with essential nutrients. It is imperative to segregate food scraps from other waste and utilise designated compost containers or systems to ensure efficient decomposition and minimise landfill impact. Furthermore, practising portion control, making informed grocery choices to reduce surplus perishables, and repurposing leftovers contribute to a more conscientious approach to food waste management.

A shloka from the Taittiriya Upanishad resonates with this sentiment, '*annam na nindyāt, tadvratam*' [Resolve not to waste food].

Mindful Eating

Mindful eating is about paying attention to what you are eating, eating slowly, and enjoying each bite. It helps you listen to your body's hunger and fullness cues for you to make healthier choices and avoid eating out of boredom or emotions. Mindful eating can improve digestion, help with weight management, and make you feel better overall. When you practise mindful eating, you focus on finding a balance between what your mind wants and your body needs. It involves being aware of when you're hungry and what you're craving.

Some tips for mindful eating:

a. **Shedding Ancestral Habits:** The first step is to start by shedding any ancestral habits that may be influencing your current relationship with food. Your ancestors' eating habits may not align with your body's needs, thus, it's essential to make choices based on what's best for you. Professionals can help you determine the best eating approach for your individual needs, as what works for one person may not work for another. Focus on creating a healthy connection between your brain and gut to make informed choices about your diet.

b. **Gratitude and Awareness:** Being grateful for the food you have and the ability to enjoy it is key to mindful eating. It helps you appreciate every aspect of your meal and be more aware of what you're putting inside your body.

c. **Listening to Your Body:** Pay attention to your body's signals and cues. Eat when you're truly hungry, chew your food thoroughly, and stop eating when you're about half full. This will help with digestion and prevent overeating.

d. **Avoiding Emotional Eating:** Resist eating out of emotions like anger or sadness. Focus on the flavours and textures of your food to truly enjoy your meal.

Thích Nhất Hạnh wrote, 'Spend time with your food; every minute of your meal should be happy. Not many people have the time and the opportunity to sit down and enjoy a meal like that. We are very fortunate.'

Mindful Bathing

Take a moment to appreciate the sensation of the water as it touches your head, and flows down your face, lips, and body, eventually reaching the floor. It is a privilege to have access to clean, temperature-controlled water that flows freely, and we should be grateful for this luxury. Additionally, having a clean, warm, and cosy towel waiting for us after our bath to dry and comfort us is a simple pleasure that we should appreciate each day.

Incorporating mindfulness into our bathing routine can help us to fully appreciate and savour the experience, turning a simple act of hygiene into a moment of relaxation and self-care.

After bathing, it is important to properly moisturise your body with a natural moisturiser. Be sure to apply the moisturiser to your face, neck, body, and legs, as well as your fingers and toes. Furthermore, pay attention to the texture of your hair as you comb it with your fingers. Keep an eye out for any signs of cracked feet, dry skin, or other issues that may require attention.

Cleaning the orifices of the body, such as the ears, nose, and genitals, is an important aspect of personal hygiene that should be done regularly while bathing. For the ears, gently cleaning around the outer ear with a washcloth is sufficient to remove excess wax and debris. Avoid inserting anything into the ear canal to prevent damage. For the nose, embrace the *Jal Neti* practice, gently blowing your nose and using a saline solution to help clear any mucus or blockages. When it comes to cleaning genital orifices, use a mild soap and warm water to cleanse the area thoroughly. Remember to always practise proper hygiene techniques by washing your hands before and after cleaning these sensitive areas to prevent infections or further complications.

According to the Ayurvedic ancient text, Charaka Samhita, 'Bathing is purifying, life promoting, a destroyer of fatigue, physically removes sweat and dirt, is resuscitative and a promoter of ojas or divine energy.'

Mindful Sleeping

A thorough search on the Internet yields ample evidence of

the numerous benefits of quality sleep. While delving into the specifics of these benefits may be unnecessary, it is crucial to recognise the profound connection between sleep and mindfulness. Individuals are more aware today of the need for adequate sleep, but there is immense pressure to prioritise sleep, leading to added stress surrounding the act of sleeping itself.

Just as the amount of water required by the body varies on weight and constitution, the optimal number of hours of restful sleep is unique to each individual. Understanding the body's capacity to handle daily tasks is essential in determining whether one's sleep is sufficient. Mindfulness practices play a significant role in this regard, as they heighten awareness of the symptoms of inadequate sleep and facilitate necessary adjustments to restore the body's energy levels.

Travelling across time zones often results in experiencing jet lag. Similarly, a night of poor sleep can leave you feeling jet-lagged the next morning. Consistently being sleep-deprived can weaken your immune system and increase the risk of various illnesses. Prioritising quality sleep improves overall well-being and enhances mindfulness by allowing the body to rest and rejuvenate effectively.

Many of us struggle to fall asleep due to the racing thoughts that occupy our minds. In an attempt to combat this, we often turn to visual stimulation, such as phones, TVs, or computers, in hopes of inducing sleep. However, this approach typically has the opposite effect, leaving us even more sleep-deprived.

To improve our sleep quality, it is advisable to eliminate all forms of visual stimuli at least an hour before bedtime. Engaging in meditation practices like body scan meditation or guided meditation can be highly beneficial in helping the body unwind. Connecting our thoughts with our breath is probably one of the best-known ways to effectively prepare ourselves for a restful night's sleep.

Mindful Economics

In today's digital age, we are inundated with conflicting messages about the economy, leading to fear and impulsive decision-making. Social media algorithms significantly shape consumer behaviour, but it's crucial to discern valuable insights from mere chatter. To navigate this chaos, we must cultivate a mindset of acceptance and shield ourselves from external triggers and social media noise. By focusing on self-awareness and desensitising ourselves to external influences, we can navigate the ever-changing global economy with resilience and adaptability.

Understanding the historical beliefs surrounding money within our family lineage can transform our financial situation. Reflecting on our ancestors' financial strategies during challenges, abundance, and retirement planning can provide insights into our own financial goals. By being mindful of our financial situation without feeling overwhelmed, setting clear financial goals, and making informed choices, we can achieve financial stability and confidence in managing our finances. Ultimately, self-awareness and mindfulness in our financial decisions can lead us towards financial success and a balanced approach to managing our resources.

Mindful Cleaning

On my first trip abroad, I distinctly remember missing the household help in India, who assisted with cleaning, more than my friends or family. Recognising that I was among the privileged few not only filled me with gratitude but also made me realise the need to be extremely organised with my time and energy to fit cleaning into my daily schedule.

Over the years, as I fine-tuned my daily routine, I realised that cleaning doesn't need to be a mindless chore—it can be an opportunity for mindfulness and presence. By incorporating mindfulness into your cleaning routine, you can transform a mundane task into a meditative practice.

Beyond aesthetics, a clean environment can significantly benefit our mental health. Cleaning provides a sense of control and calm in an otherwise chaotic world. A clutter-free workspace can enhance concentration levels, and a clearer physical environment can lead to a sharper mind, allowing for better thinking.

In today's world, it is more important than ever to consider the environmental impact of our cleaning habits. By choosing eco-friendly cleaning products and methods, we can reduce our carbon footprint and contribute to a healthier planet. Biodegradable, non-toxic, and cruelty-free products ensure that your cleaning routine is effective and environmentally conscious.

Mindful Socialising

Mindfulness is a powerful tool that helps you carefully choose the individuals you allow into your life. This intentional selection can deeply impact your well-being and overall happiness.

The essence of mindfulness lies in strengthening your emotional resilience, enabling you to exude self-confidence while navigating various insecurities—whether financial, emotional, or physical. By practising mindfulness, you can free your mind from negative thoughts and embrace your authentic self on your own terms.

While human connection is essential in a society that thrives on interdependence, it is equally important to establish boundaries regarding the level of interaction you engage in. Consider how much influence you allow others to have on your decisions, and carefully select which aspects of society you choose to embrace. By being mindful of these choices, you can cultivate a sense of empowerment and autonomy in your life.

Mindfulness with the Self

Mindfulness offers a profound benefit by providing a deeper understanding of oneself, including boundaries and limitations—physical, emotional, and mental. It grants permission to prioritise one's own needs over those of others.

Generosity, magnanimity, and compassion are some of the qualities that reflect a person's willingness to offer their time and resources selflessly. While commendable, there is a term for individuals who are overly generous yet struggle to accept anything in return—people-pleasers. Deep-seated feelings of insecurity and inadequacy can lead to a constant need for validation and approval, resulting in an over-giving mentality.

The practice of mindfulness and self-awareness is essential in addressing compulsive behaviour. By promoting mindfulness and increasing the self-awareness of our emotions, we can recognise warning signs of over-giving. The key to overcoming over-giving is to practise self-compassion and holistically accept ourselves. Just as flight attendants instruct passengers to secure their own oxygen masks before assisting others, it is crucial to prioritise self-care daily. Embracing mindfulness and self-awareness allows us to understand and address our behaviours, leading to a healthier and more balanced approach to giving and receiving.

Maintaining authenticity in the face of societal pressures is a true testament to one's mindfulness journey. It is not about how others perceive us, instead, it involves how we perceive ourselves when we go against our own beliefs or values. Managing emotions and relationships is both a science and an art. While the theory may seem simple, the actual practice of managing emotions is complex and nuanced.

Creating thoughtful responses, instead of reacting impulsively, allows us to become masters of our own words and actions. This process is challenging and rewarding, requiring us to navigate the intricacies of human interaction with grace and intention. Embracing this experience as an opportunity for growth and self-discovery is essential.

Every individual who comes into our lives serves a purpose—whether for a reason, a season, or a lifetime. It's important to practise gratitude for their presence and accept their impact on us. Even those who have spoken ill of us can teach us valuable lessons in strength and self-awareness. It may be challenging, but we must thank them for these lessons and then let them go, even if it means distancing ourselves from them. What doesn't break us makes us stronger, and by acknowledging and releasing negative thoughts, we can move forward with a greater understanding and appreciation for the people and experiences in our lives.

Building Meaningful Relationships through Mindfulness

When you begin your journey into mindfulness, you may find that you no longer relate to certain individuals. Their beliefs and habits might not align with your own, making you feel like an outsider in the society you have always known. However, mindfulness can help alleviate these feelings of insecurity and restore your confidence in your choices. It teaches you that you do not need validation or approval from others, as long as your intentions are genuine and purposeful.

Over time, mindfulness can also reduce social anxiety. By recognising and acknowledging the reasons behind our social discomfort, we can set those feelings aside for later reflection and simply enjoy the present moment. With mindfulness, you can appreciate that everyone is entitled to their own choices without passing judgment.

By approaching such situations with a sense of lightness and humour, you can navigate social interactions more smoothly. Instead of feeling alienated or defensive, you can engage in conversations with an open mind and a willingness to learn from others. Mindfulness helps you in letting go of preconceived notions and embracing the diversity of perspectives around you, creating a more relaxed and enjoyable social environment.

After labelling your thoughts, take the time to reflect on why you felt anxious in that moment. Was it due to concerns about how a peer might perceive your financial status? Or perhaps it stemmed from a need for validation that you struggle to overcome? By practising kindness and compassion towards yourself, you can combat these judgmental thoughts and regain your confidence.

Remember, the only narrative that truly matters is the one you tell yourself.

This quote from *Chanakya Neeti* serves as a reminder to carefully evaluate various aspects of your life, make informed decisions, and maintain a sense of empowerment:

> kaḥ kālaḥ kāni mitrāṇi ko deśaḥ kau vyayāgamau ।
> kaścāhaṃ kā ca me śaktiriti cintyaṃ muhurmuhuḥ ॥

> [Consider again and again the following: the right time, the right friends, the right place, the right means of income, the right ways of spending, and from whom you derive your power.]

17
Decluttering Your Mind and Space

'Out of clutter, find simplicity. From discord, find harmony. In the middle of difficulty lies opportunity.'
—Albert Einstein

Individuals need to declutter their minds and physical spaces to maintain focus, productivity, and overall well-being. By organising one's thoughts and eliminating mental clutter, individuals can better prioritise tasks, problem-solve efficiently, and make well-informed decisions. This can be achieved through practices such as mindfulness meditation, journalling, or creating to-do lists. Similarly, decluttering one's physical space by removing unnecessary items, establishing an organisational system, and maintaining a clean work environment can minimise distractions and promote a clear mind.

When faced with clutter, whether physical or mental, it can be challenging to navigate the chaos. However, by decluttering and organising our surroundings, we can create a sense of calm and order. Similarly, when discord arises in our relationships or environments, we can strive to find common ground and work towards harmony.

Marie Kondo, a renowned Japanese decluttering consultant, has developed the 'KonMari Method' as a systematic approach to tidying up. It emphasises organising belongings by category and keeping only items that 'spark joy'. By following this method, we can create a space that is not only clean and organised but also brings us joy and peace.

While we may not all be professional decluttering consultants like Marie Kondo, we can still learn from her approach and apply it to our own lives. By clearing our minds and physical spaces of unnecessary clutter, we can create a more peaceful and harmonious environment for ourselves. Let us take inspiration from those who find joy in decluttering and create simplicity and harmony in our own lives.

This combination of mental and physical decluttering allows individuals to operate at their highest potential by reducing stress, increasing efficiency, and fostering a sense of clarity that leads to improved performance in everything they choose to do.

The Science behind Getting Things Cleaned Up

Imagine walking into a cluttered room that you have been avoiding for several days. The reason for avoiding it is the emotions you knew you would have to face once you entered. However, decluttering can provide a sense of order, even when the task seems overwhelming. It allows us to feel in control of our surroundings and promotes mindfulness as we focus on organising and achieving a goal.

Emotions like anger, frustration, and disbelief may arise when faced with clutter initially. These emotions can lead to stress, triggering the release of cortisol. Living in a state of chaos and clutter over time can result in long-term negative feelings, such as sadness. The inability to address the clutter can also lead to shame and guilt, as they may prevent us from inviting others into our homes. Furthermore, the impact of clutter extends beyond emotions, affecting our physical health as well.

Sleep loss and various physical issues can arise from living in a cluttered environment.

It is important to recognise the negative effects of clutter and take steps to address it. By decluttering and organising our spaces, we can create a more positive and inviting environment. Mindfully putting things back where they belong can help us regain control and achieve a sense of accomplishment. Let us shift our focus towards tidying up our thoughts and finding a positive spin on the negative consequences of clutter.

The Art of Getting Things Cleaned Up

Having experienced moving to various continents and residing in multiple residences, the concept of packing up and relocating is familiar to me. As someone who has consistently moved to different corners of the globe, the comfort of surrounding myself with familiar objects that hold sentimental value is truly unmatched. This practice has allowed me to feel a sense of 'home' even in foreign lands, transforming what was once considered a tedious task into a truly enjoyable experience.

Awareness of the body and mind in creating an aesthetically pleasing and functional home is an art of mindfulness that can be worked on even if you do not possess a creative gene.

Awareness of feelings, as the other foundation of mindfulness, is achieved by balancing the requirements of all family members to ensure that their needs are met. It must be done in a non-judgmental manner.

Awareness of Dharma is accomplished by finding the use—the right people or organisations—for things you do not need.

Repurposing old furniture and sentimental items to serve a new function can be an incredibly fulfilling endeavour, requiring a discerning eye to distinguish between what is essential and what is superfluous. Through careful planning and thoughtful consideration of our needs, we can create living spaces that are not only aesthetically pleasing but also welcoming in a holistic sense. By embracing these principles of mindfulness in home design, we can cultivate a sense of peace and harmony within our living spaces.

18
The Power of Doing Nothing

'Don't underestimate the value of doing nothing, of just going along, listening to all the things you can't hear, and not bothering.'

—A. A. Milne

Many of us have been scolded as adolescents by our parents for lounging around and not being productive. 'Get up and do something,' they would often say. I reflect on those carefree days when I could simply listen to music or do nothing at all. However, as adults, it is challenging to resist the urge to constantly stay busy and quiet the racing thoughts.

The incessant need to always be doing something, meeting the demands of society, and striving to achieve numerous goals in a short time can be likened to a disease. It is a disease of the mind, driven by a desire to feel valued and relevant. It is a disease of society that imposes these expectations. It is a disease of seeking validation and love from others. If left unaddressed, these pressures can manifest as physical ailments.

The power of doing nothing does not lie in the absence of thoughts but in the ability to channel and embrace them. We can find peace by allowing our minds to wander freely without the pressure of achieving something. Just as fasting allows our cells to rejuvenate, giving ourselves the gift of doing nothing lets our brain process emotions and experiences.

This state of rest is important for emotional regulation. By creating a mental library of positive experiences, we can reduce the fight-or-flight response triggered by the amygdala. This, in turn, helps to alleviate stress and promote emotional well-being.

For those accustomed to constant activity, the idea of doing nothing may seem exhausting. The fear of missing out or not being productive can lead to feelings of overwhelm. However, disconnecting from technology and engaging in activities like reading can significantly reduce stress levels.

To keep your mind engaged, it is important to practise certain techniques:

a. Intentionally put your phone away and take in your surroundings.
b. Focus on a single object for approximately two minutes, clearing your mind of any distractions. If thoughts arise, redirect your attention back to the object in front of you.

Historically, lighting lamps were used to enhance focus during meditation, while burning incense sticks helped eliminate unpleasant odours that could disrupt thoughts. This concept forms the basis of ritualistic or visual meditation, which was discussed earlier as a valuable tool for enhancing observation skills and increasing awareness of our surroundings, including signals from our own bodies.

Doing nothing, or embracing periods of stillness and rest, offers a range of benefits for both mental and physical health:

a. Reduces Stress: Taking time to do nothing helps lower cortisol levels, reducing overall stress and promoting relaxation.

b. Enhances Creativity: Periods of inactivity allow the mind to wander, which can lead to creative insights and problem-solving.

3. **Improves Mental Clarity**: Taking breaks from constant activity helps clear mental clutter, improving focus and cognitive function.
4. **Boosts Emotional Well-being**: Rest and relaxation can improve mood and emotional resilience by providing time to recharge and reflect.
5. **Promotes Physical Health**: Regular rest can lower blood pressure, reduce the risk of chronic diseases, and support overall physical recovery.
6. **Encourages Self-Awareness**: Moments of stillness allow for introspection, helping individuals gain insights into their thoughts, feelings, and motivations.
7. **Fosters Better Sleep**: Taking time to rest during the day can improve nighttime sleep quality by reducing overall stress and fatigue.
8. **Increases Productivity**: Periods of doing nothing can prevent burnout and improve productivity by ensuring that when you do work, you're more focused and efficient.
9. **Strengthens Relationships**: Being present and relaxed can improve interpersonal interactions, as it allows for more meaningful connections and communication.
10. **Enhances Mindfulness**: Doing nothing provides an opportunity to practise mindfulness, nurturing a deeper awareness of the present moment.

Including periods of doing nothing into your routine can lead to a more balanced and fulfilling life, enhancing overall well-being and effectiveness.

19
Overcoming Struggles with Mindfulness

The struggles of modern life can take a toll on our mental and emotional well-being. This chapter offers a gentle yet powerful approach to navigating life's difficulties. By consistently practising mindfulness, you can cultivate a deeper sense of awareness, calm, and resilience. These exercises are designed to help you reconnect with yourself, find balance, and face your struggles with a renewed sense of clarity and peace.

Mindfulness Exercise to Increase Gratitude

The cornerstone of mindfulness is gratitude, serving as a foundation for cultivating awareness and appreciation for the present moment. By acknowledging and being thankful for the blessings in our lives, we can shift our focus from negativity to positivity, fostering a more peaceful and content state of mind. Practising gratitude also helps us develop resilience and perspective, enabling us to navigate challenges with grace and acceptance.

While often perceived as a simple concept, maintaining a mindset of gratitude requires intentional effort and self-awareness, especially amidst the chaos and stress of work. It involves shifting focus from what is lacking or going wrong to appreciating what is going well and expressing genuine thanks for it. Developing a habit of gratitude takes practice, patience, and perseverance, particularly when faced with setbacks or unfavourable circumstances.

Here are some techniques you can practise regularly, so they become second nature and can be used as tools during difficult times:

- **Gratitude Journalling:** Set aside a few moments each day to write in a journal. List three to five things you are thankful for, focusing on specific moments or experiences. Reflect on why these things matter to you and how they enhance your life. Regularly revisit your entries to reinforce a grateful mindset.
- **Gratitude Meditation:** Find a quiet spot and sit comfortably. Close your eyes and take a few deep breaths to centre yourself. Think of someone or something for which you are grateful. Visualise this person or thing and focus on the positive feelings it evokes.
- **Gratitude Walk:** Take a walk in a natural setting or around your neighbourhood. As you walk, pay attention to the sights, sounds, and smells around you. Be thankful for the things you see and experience, such as the beauty of nature or the kindness of strangers.
- **Gratitude Visualisation:** Relax in your seat and close your eyes. Picture a situation or experience where you felt deeply grateful. Visualise the specifics of this experience, such as the people involved and the positive emotions you felt. Allow yourself to fully immerse in these feelings of appreciation.
- **Mindful Appreciation:** Choose an everyday object or experience, such as a meal, a favourite mug, or a moment of quiet. Be mindful of it, focusing on its qualities and how it enriches your life. Reflect on why you value it and how it contributes to your well-being. Practise this regularly to cultivate a deeper appreciation for ordinary moments.

- **Gratitude Reflection:** At the end of each day, take a few moments to reflect on your day. Think of three things you are thankful for from that day. Consider how each of these things positively impacted your life and how you can carry this sense of gratitude into the next day.
- **Gratitude Letter:** Write a letter to someone you appreciate, expressing your gratitude for their impact on your life. Be specific about what you are thankful for and how it has affected you. You can choose to send the letter or keep it as a reminder of your appreciation. This activity helps strengthen your appreciation for others and deepens your connection with them.
- **Mindful Eating with Gratitude:** Before eating, take a moment to appreciate the food in front of you. Notice the colours, textures, and aromas of the food. Reflect on the effort and resources that went into preparing the meal, including the people involved. Eat slowly, savouring each bite, and express gratitude for the nourishment it provides.
- **Gratitude Affirmations:** Choose a few affirmations related to gratitude, such as 'I am grateful for the abundance in my life' or 'I appreciate the kindness of others.' Silently or aloud, say these affirmations to yourself. Focus on the meaning of each affirmation and let it resonate within you. Practise this regularly to reinforce a grateful mindset.
- **Gratitude Sharing:** Share something you are thankful for with a friend, family member, or colleague. Discuss why you feel grateful and how it has positively impacted your life. Invite the other person to share their own gratitude, creating a shared exchange of appreciation. This practice strengthens connections and spreads positive emotions.

Adopt one or more of these mindfulness exercises to embrace mindfulness in every walk of life.

Mindfulness Exercises to Improve Concentration

Improving concentration and attention is crucial to emotional well-being, as it directly impacts productivity and efficiency. To enhance these cognitive skills, individuals can adopt various strategies, such as setting specific goals, creating a structured environment with minimal distractions, practising mindfulness techniques like meditation or deep breathing exercises, getting adequate sleep to ensure optimal brain function, staying hydrated throughout the day to maintain focus, and taking short breaks during intensive tasks to prevent mental burnout. Regular physical exercise has also been shown to boost cognitive abilities and overall brain health.

One highly effective mindfulness activity for improving concentration is Focused Attention Meditation. Regularly practising this meditation can significantly enhance your ability to concentrate, leading to improved performance in various areas of your life.

- **Choose a Quiet Space:** Find a quiet, comfortable place where you won't be disturbed. Sit in a comfortable position with your back straight and your hands resting on your lap or knees.
- **Set a Timer:** Decide on the duration of your practice, starting with 5 to 10 minutes if you're new to meditation. You can gradually increase this time as you become more comfortable.
- **Focus on Your Breath:** Close your eyes or lower your gaze. Take a few deep breaths, inhaling through your nose and exhaling through your mouth. Allow yourself to relax with each breath. Choose a specific aspect of your breath to focus on, such as the sensation of air entering and leaving your nostrils, the rise and fall of your abdomen, or the sound of your breath.

- **Maintain Your Focus and Redirect Attention:** As you focus on your breath, thoughts and distractions will inevitably arise. When you notice your mind wandering, gently bring your attention back to your chosen focal point. Acknowledge distractions without judgment and calmly redirect your focus to your breath.
- **Use a Focal Object:** If focusing on your breath feels challenging, you can use a physical object like a candle flame or a small stone as your focal point. Gaze softly at the object or visualise it in your mind, maintaining your attention on its details.
- **Practice Mindful Noticing:** Pay attention to the physical sensations associated with your chosen focus. Notice how your breath feels as it flows in and out or observe the textures and colours of the object you're focusing on. Continuously bring your attention back to these sensations whenever you become aware of distractions.
- **End with Reflection:** When the timer goes off, take a few moments to notice how you feel. Observe any changes in your state of mind or concentration.
- **Integrate Mindfulness into Daily Tasks:** Practise bringing the focused attention you've developed into daily activities, such as reading, working, or conversations. Apply the same principles of maintaining attention and gently redirecting distractions.

Mindfulness Exercises to Overcome Loneliness

Loneliness, often experienced as a lack of meaningful social connections or a sense of isolation, can have detrimental effects on mental and physical well-being. In contrast, solitude is the state of being alone without feeling lonely. While loneliness negatively impacts mental health, solitude can be rejuvenating, allowing individuals to recharge, gain clarity, and engage in self-reflection and personal growth.

To overcome feelings of loneliness, a mindfulness activity that can be particularly effective is 'Compassionate Self-Connection.' This practice focuses on nurturing a compassionate relationship with yourself and fostering a sense of connection and self-care.

- **Focus on Your Breath:** Choose a comfortable spot, close your eyes or soften your gaze, and take several deep, calming breaths. Inhale through your nose, hold for a moment, and exhale slowly through your mouth, settling into the present moment.
- **Acknowledge Your Feelings (Recognise Loneliness):** Gently bring to mind the feelings of loneliness you're experiencing, acknowledging them without judgment. Notice any emotions or thoughts associated with loneliness, recognising that these feelings are temporary.
- **Practise Self-Compassion (Place a Hand on Your Heart):** Rest one or both hands over your heart. This physical gesture can provide comfort and a sense of connection. Silently or aloud, speak to yourself with compassion and understanding, using phrases such as: 'It's okay to feel lonely; I am here for myself. I am doing my best, and I am enough just as I am.' Alternatively, chant the mantra, *Aham Brahmasmi*, which means 'I am the Universe' or 'I am part of the Divine.' This concept implies that everyone possesses a unique essence interconnected with the cosmos, serving as a powerful reminder of the limitless possibilities within us.
- **Identify Self-Care Activities**: Think about activities that bring you joy and comfort, such as reading a favourite book, taking a warm bath, or listening to soothing music. Plan to engage in one or more of these self-care activities.

- **Reflect on Positive Connections:** Reflect on past positive interactions or relationships where you felt connected and valued. Consider what made those connections meaningful and how you might reach out to those who made you feel good.
- **Return to the Present:** Gently bring your focus back to the present moment. Take a few deep breaths and gradually open your eyes.

Mindfulness Exercises for Emotional Resilience

Emotional resilience entails the ability to regulate one's emotions, maintain a positive outlook, and recover from adversity with strength and renewed determination. Those who are emotionally resilient possess a strong sense of self-awareness, effectively manage stress, and can seek support and utilise healthy coping mechanisms during difficult times. To enhance emotional resilience or overcome feelings of powerlessness, a particularly effective mindfulness activity is 'Empowerment Visualisation.' This activity focuses on recognising your strengths and potential, fostering a sense of empowerment and control.

- **Find a Comfortable Space:** Sit or lie down in a quiet, comfortable space where you can focus without distractions.
- **Ground Yourself:** Take a few deep breaths to centre yourself. Inhale deeply through your nose, hold for a moment, and exhale slowly through your mouth. Allow your body to relax with each breath.
- **Visualise Your Strengths:** Picture a place where you feel completely safe and secure, whether a real location or an imagined one. Imagine a source of energy or power

within you, represented by a glowing light, a powerful symbol, or an inspiring figure. Visualise this source of power growing stronger and brighter.

- **Reflect on Personal Achievements:** Recall moments when you felt strong, capable, or successful. Visualise these experiences vividly, focusing on how you felt during those times. Recognise and affirm your personal strengths and abilities.
- **Empowerment Affirmations:** Silently or aloud, repeat affirmations that reinforce your sense of power and control, such as: 'I am capable and strong', 'I have the power to create positive change in my life', and 'I trust in my abilities and make confident decisions.'
- **Envision Future Goals:** Picture yourself successfully achieving your current goals or overcoming challenges. See yourself taking proactive steps and feeling empowered in the process. Embrace the feelings of accomplishment and control.
- **Return to the Present:** Gradually bring your focus back to the present moment. Take a few deep breaths and gently open your eyes or lift your gaze. After the visualisation, reflect on how you can apply the sense of empowerment you've cultivated to real-life situations.

Mindfulness Exercise to Improve Communication

Effective communication is essential in any setting – professional or personal. It sets the foundation for building trust, fostering positive relationships, and ensuring clarity of expectations between individuals. Misunderstandings between family members and friends are commonplace and most often stem from misunderstood thoughts and actions that arise from misplaced expectations.

Good communication involves conveying information clearly and concisely and actively listening to others and engaging in meaningful dialogue. According to psychologist Albert Mehrabian, the 7-38-55 rule states that 7 per cent of communication is conveyed by our words, 38 per cent comes via our tone of voice, and 55 per cent comes through body language. A mindfulness activity to enhance and control communication is 'mindful listening and speaking practice.' There are many ways that you can practice listening and speaking. Some simple suggestions are given below.

- **Set the Intention:** Before starting a conversation or communication, set the intention to be fully present and mindful. Remind yourself to listen deeply and speak with awareness.
- **Mindful Listening:** When someone is speaking to you, give them your full attention. Avoid interrupting or thinking about your response while they are talking. Pay attention to the speaker's body language, tone of voice, and facial expressions. After the speaker has finished, briefly reflect on what you heard. You can paraphrase or summarise their main points to ensure you have understood them correctly.
- **Mindful Speaking:** Before responding, take a brief pause to collect your thoughts. This pause allows you to respond thoughtfully rather than react impulsively. Choose your words carefully to convey your message clearly and respectfully. Avoid using language that could be interpreted as judgmental or aggressive. Ensure your message is being understood as intended. You can ask open-ended questions or seek feedback to confirm that your communication is effective.
- **Practice Empathy:** Be aware of both your emotions and the emotions of the person you are communicating with.

Acknowledge feelings and respond with empathy and compassion. Show understanding and respect for the other person's viewpoint, even if you disagree. Validating their perspective can foster a more open and constructive dialogue.

- **Reflect on the Interaction:** After the conversation, take a moment to reflect on how it went. Consider what aspects of your communication were effective and what could be improved by reflecting on your own mindfulness during the interaction.

Mindfulness Exercises to Practise Detachment

Detachment can be cultivated through mindfulness techniques, consciously recognising the impermanence of all things and accepting change as a natural part of life. A mindfulness activity that fosters emotional balance and is particularly effective for detaching from outcomes, expectations, and attachments—whether to material possessions or relationships—is the 'Mindful Detachment Practice.'

- **Focus on Your Breath:** Sit or lie down comfortably. Close your eyes or soften your gaze. Take a few deep breaths, directing your attention to the sensation of breathing.
- **Identify the Source of Attachment:** Gently bring to mind the person, object, or situation to which you feel overly attached. Observe the associated thoughts and emotions.
- **Observe Without Judgment:** Fully experience the feelings and thoughts related to the attachment. Observe them as they arise, recognising that these feelings are temporary and do not define you.

- **Practise the 'Letting Go' Visualisation:** Visualise the object of your attachment as a leaf floating down a stream. Watch it drift away, and with each breath, let go of your hold on it, allowing it to flow freely.
- **Use Detachment Affirmations:** Repeat gentle affirmations to support your practice. Examples include: 'I release my need to control and allow things to unfold naturally' or chant the Sanskrit mantra *Idam Na Mama*, meaning 'This is not mine.' These simple words are a powerful affirmation of surrender.
- **Return to the Present Moment:** Refocus on your breath or bodily sensations. Remind yourself that you are grounded in the present moment, separate from the attachment.
- **Reflect on Your Experience:** Spend a few moments reflecting on the practice. Notice any changes in your emotional state or perspective on the attachment.
- **Practise Self-Compassion:** Acknowledge that it is natural to have attachments and that learning to let go is a process. Treat yourself with kindness and patience as you work through these feelings.

Mindfulness Exercises to Overcome Anxiety or Overthinking

Anxiety and overthinking are common challenges that many people face, often leading to a cycle of negative thoughts and emotions that can be difficult to overcome. However, several effective strategies exist for managing these obstacles. One approach is mindfulness, which involves staying present in the moment rather than dwelling on the past or worrying about the future. Mindfulness practices such as meditation and deep breathing can help calm the mind and reduce anxiety levels.

Cognitive-behavioural therapy (CBT) is another effective technique that focuses on challenging and changing negative thought patterns to promote a more balanced and rational response to stressors. Additionally, regular exercise, sufficient sleep, and a healthy diet are vital in managing anxiety and overthinking. By taking proactive steps and implementing coping strategies, individuals can gradually gain control over their thoughts and emotions, leading to greater peace and stability in their daily lives.

One effective mindfulness activity for combating overthinking is 'Thought Labelling', which involves recognising and labelling intrusive thoughts to detach from them and remain focused on the present moment. Practising these strategies can help individuals break free from the cycle of overthinking and anxiety, leading to greater mental well-being.

- **Find a Quiet Space:** Sit comfortably in a quiet area where you can focus without distractions.
- **Notice Your Thoughts:** Close your eyes or lower your gaze and observe your thoughts as they arise. Try not to engage with them; simply notice them.
- **Label the Thoughts:** As each thought appears, gently label it with a descriptive term, such as 'worry', 'planning', 'judgment', or 'memory.' For example, if you think about a future event, label it 'planning.'
- **Return to the Present:** After labelling a thought, gently bring your attention to your breath or a calming focal point. You can use a simple mantra like 'Here and now' to help refocus.
- **Repeat as Necessary:** Continue to observe and label thoughts as they arise, returning your focus to the present moment each time.

Other techniques known to help distract the mind from overthinking or feelings of overwhelm include:

- **Avoid Multitasking:** Focusing on one task at a time is beneficial. An analogy is like having many tabs open on a browser; productivity improves when you close all tabs except the one you are working on.
- **Take a Break from Electronic Devices:** Keep your phone away, take a walk, or close your eyes and listen to music that you enjoy and appreciate, which can help calm you down.
- **Breathwork:** As mentioned in previous chapters, breathwork techniques can be particularly effective.
- **Seek Professional Help:** Consult a therapist to analyse your situation and determine whether unresolved childhood issues may be influencing your current perceptions.

Mindfulness Exercises to Cope with Overwhelm or Stress

Stress and overwhelm are common experiences that affect everyone. When individuals feel overwhelmed, their ability to think clearly and perform effectively may be compromised, leading to decreased productivity, burnout, and even physical health issues such as headaches or insomnia. By recognising the signs of stress early on and taking steps to address them, we can protect our well-being and foster more sustainable living.

Mindfulness-based cognitive therapy (MBCT) is a therapeutic approach that combines mindfulness practices with cognitive therapy principles to help individuals manage symptoms of depression, anxiety, and other mental health issues. By teaching clients to become more present in the moment, MBCT aims to increase awareness of thoughts and feelings, helping them develop healthier coping mechanisms and reduce the impact of negative thought patterns. Developed by Zindel Segal, Mark Williams, and John Teasdale, MBCT is derived from the earlier work of Teasdale, Jon Kabat-Zinn, and Phillip Barnard.

MBCT helps individuals understand what depression is, discover what makes them vulnerable to downward mood spirals, and why they get stuck at the bottom of the spiral. It helps them see the connection between downward spirals and the high standards that oppress them or feelings of not being 'good enough.' MBCT also aids in identifying ways individuals put pressure on themselves or make themselves miserable with overwork, and it helps them reconnect with what makes life worth living. MBCT is best practised with a certified professional trained to identify problems and suggest appropriate remedial measures.

One MBCT technique is the three-minute breathing space, a mindfulness practice that grounds individuals in the present moment. It involves three distinct steps: first, acknowledging current thoughts, emotions, and bodily sensations without judgment; second, focusing on the sensations of breathing and taking slow, intentional breaths to centre oneself; and finally, expanding awareness to the body as a whole and the surrounding environment.

Another technique is mindful stretching, which can be practised daily:

- **Pandiculation:** A mindful stretch that can be practised every morning. Place palms on your shoulders, raise the elbows, and yawn. This reflexive action increases blood flow, releases tension, and improves overall muscle function.
- **Yoga Poses:** Do stretching asanas.
- **Proprioceptive Neuromuscular Facilitation (PNF) techniques:** These stretching and strengthening exercises, used by healthcare professionals, improve flexibility, strength, and coordination. Research indicates

that PNF positively affects the active and passive range of emotions.[6]

Mindfulness-based interventions such as Mindfulness-Based Stress Reduction (MBSR) and MBCT promote a major shift in mindset, resulting in greater emotional regulation, improved self-awareness, and enhanced ability to cope with stressors. By cultivating non-judgmental awareness of thoughts, emotions, and bodily sensations, individuals can develop a more balanced perspective on their experiences and respond to them more adaptively. This mindfulness practice is thought to promote psychological well-being by fostering acceptance, compassion, and resilience in the face of life's challenges.

Mindfulness Exercises to Improve Self-Esteem

Individuals with high self-esteem are more likely to take on challenges, speak up in public, and pursue growth opportunities. They handle criticism and setbacks better, viewing them as opportunities for learning rather than personal failures. Those with healthy self-esteem tend to have more successful relationships and excel in their chosen pursuits. Mindfulness exercises can be powerful tools for improving self-esteem by helping you develop a more compassionate, accepting, and realistic view of yourself. Here are some mindfulness practices designed to enhance self-esteem:

- **Surround Yourself with the Right Company:** The company we keep during vulnerable times greatly

6. Lindsay J. Hoffman and William L. Schrader, 'Proprioceptive Neuromuscular Facilitation: Mechanisms and Clinical Implications,' *Journal of Manual & Manipulative Therapy* 19, no. 1 (2011): 19–27, https://www.ncbi.nlm.nih.gov/pmc/articles/PMC3588663/.

influences our ability to overcome challenges. Surround yourself with people who genuinely care about your well-being. It's important to avoid not only naysayers but also those who may unintentionally hinder your journey toward self-love.

- **Seek Professional Help:** If small measures are not effective, consider consulting a therapist. You may need someone to hold you accountable or validate your efforts. If low self-esteem stems from body image issues, seek specialised help to address these concerns systematically.
- **Loving-Kindness Meditation:** Sit comfortably, close your eyes, and take a few deep breaths. Silently repeat phrases of loving-kindness to yourself, such as 'May I be happy, may I be healthy, may I be safe, may I be at peace.' Allow yourself to genuinely feel the kindness and compassion you are offering. Continue for 5-10 minutes, letting go of self-criticism and embracing self-love.
- **Mindful Affirmations:** Choose affirmations that resonate with you, such as 'I am worthy of love and respect', 'I accept myself as I am', or 'I am enough.' Sit in a quiet space, close your eyes, and take a few deep breaths. Slowly repeat your affirmations, either aloud or in your mind. Focus on the meaning of each word, allowing the positive energy to take root. Practise this daily to reinforce a positive self-image.
- **Body Scan with Self-Compassion:** Lie down or sit comfortably and close your eyes. Begin by bringing attention to your toes and gradually move up your body, noticing each part. Offer silent gratitude and kindness to each area, such as 'Thank you for supporting me.' If you encounter tension or discomfort, acknowledge it with compassion, without judgment. This practice fosters a positive relationship with your body and enhances self-appreciation.

- **Gratitude Journalling:** Set aside a few minutes each day to reflect on qualities you appreciate about yourself. Write down three to five things you are grateful for, such as strengths, accomplishments, or personal traits. Focus on these positive aspects, reinforcing a sense of self-worth. Over time, this practice shifts your focus from self-criticism to self-appreciation.
- **Mirror Exercise:** Stand in front of a mirror and look into your eyes. Take a deep breath and smile gently at yourself. Say something kind or affirming, such as 'You are doing your best', 'You are worthy', or 'I love and accept you as you are.' This may feel uncomfortable at first, but with practice, it becomes a powerful way to build self-esteem. Spend a few moments each day cultivating self-compassion and acceptance.
- **Mindful Self-Reflection:** Sit in a quiet space and close your eyes. Reflect on a recent experience where you felt good about yourself, such as completing a task, helping someone, or being kind to yourself. Fully feel the positive emotions associated with that experience. Acknowledge your efforts and give yourself credit. This mindful reflection reinforces a positive self-view and improves overall self-esteem.
- **Reframing Negative Thoughts:** When you notice a negative thought about yourself, pause and take a deep breath. Acknowledge the thought without judgment, recognising it as just a thought, not an absolute truth. Challenge the negative thought by asking, 'Is this really true?' or 'What evidence contradicts this thought?' Replace it with a more balanced perspective, such as 'I made a mistake, but that doesn't define me.' Regular practice reduces self-criticism and builds healthier self-esteem.
- **Mindful Walking:** Find a quiet place to walk, whether in nature or at home. Focus on the sensation of your feet

touching the ground, your body's movement, and your breath. With each step, repeat a positive affirmation, such as 'I am worthy' or 'I trust myself.' Allow the rhythmic movement and affirmations to create a sense of inner peace and confidence, boosting self-esteem and promoting physical well-being.

By integrating one or more of these mindfulness exercises into your daily routine, you can cultivate a deeper sense of self-worth and build lasting self-esteem.

Mindfulness Exercises to Help with Forgiveness

Forgiveness is a vital part of emotional and psychological healing. Harbouring resentment, anger, or bitterness can increase stress levels, negatively affecting physical health. By choosing to forgive those who have wronged us, we free ourselves from the burden of negative emotions and allow ourselves to move forward more healthily and positively. Forgiveness fosters empathy and understanding, improving relationships and overall mental well-being. It's important to note that forgiveness does not excuse or condone harmful behaviour; it is about releasing negative emotions for our own peace of mind.

Forgiveness can be challenging, but mindfulness can support this process by cultivating awareness, compassion, and acceptance. Here are some mindfulness exercises to aid in forgiveness:

- **Loving-Kindness Meditation:** Sit comfortably and take deep breaths to centre yourself. Begin by offering loving-kindness to yourself: 'May I be happy, may I be healthy, may I be at peace.' Then, extend these wishes to someone you are struggling to forgive: 'May you be happy, may you be healthy, may you be at peace.' Finally, extend these wishes to all beings. This meditation softens the heart and encourages compassion, a key component of forgiveness.

- **Mindful Breathing with Release:** Sit in a quiet place and close your eyes. Focus on your breath, inhaling deeply and exhaling slowly. As you breathe in, imagine drawing in peace and understanding. As you exhale, visualise releasing resentment, anger, or pain. With each breath, consciously let go of the tension associated with the person or situation you want to forgive. This practice helps gradually release negative emotions and fosters inner calm.
- **Compassionate Self-Inquiry:** Find a comfortable position and take a few deep breaths to centre yourself. Reflect on the person or situation that you need to forgive. Gently ask yourself, 'What am I holding onto?' and 'How is this affecting me?' Allow any emotions to arise without judgment. Acknowledge the hurt, but also consider what you need to release this pain. This exercise encourages self-awareness and helps identify the blocks to forgiveness, allowing you to begin releasing them.
- **Body Scan for Emotional Awareness:** Lie down or sit comfortably and close your eyes. Slowly bring your attention to different parts of your body, noticing any tension or discomfort. As you scan, pay attention to areas that feel heavy or constricted—these might be places where you are holding onto resentment. Breathe into these areas, imagining the tension melting away with each exhale. This practice helps you identify where you physically hold onto anger or resentment, allowing you to consciously release it.
- **Guided Visualisation of Forgiveness:** Close your eyes and take several deep breaths. Visualise the person you

wish to forgive standing in front of you. Imagine a light or warmth emanating from your heart, enveloping both you and the other person. As the light grows, silently say to the person, 'I forgive you' or 'I am willing to forgive you', and observe how this feels in your body and mind. Visualisation can help you mentally and emotionally prepare for forgiveness, even if you're not ready to fully forgive yet.

- **Gratitude for Growth**: Sit quietly and reflect on the situation that has caused you pain. Consider any lessons or personal growth that have come from this experience, such as resilience, compassion, or a deeper understanding of yourself. Acknowledge these with gratitude, recognising how the situation, while difficult, has contributed to your development. Finding gratitude in the growth from difficult experiences can make forgiveness easier by shifting your perspective from pain to personal development.
- **Journalling with Mindful Reflection:** Set aside time to journal about your feelings towards the person or situation you are trying to forgive. Write about what happened, how it made you feel, and why you are struggling to forgive. Then, reflect on what forgiveness would mean for you. Consider how holding onto the hurt affects your life and what might change if you let it go. Writing can help you process complex emotions and gain clarity, creating mental space for forgiveness to occur.
- **Mindful Acceptance of Emotions:** Sit quietly and allow yourself to feel whatever emotions arise when you think about the person or situation you want to forgive. Don't try to push the feelings away or judge them. Observe them, labelling them if you can (e.g., anger, sadness, disappointment), and notice how they change or move through your body. This practice helps you accept and

process your emotions rather than suppressing them, which is crucial in the journey to forgiveness.

Each of these exercises can be practised regularly to cultivate the mindset and emotional resilience needed for forgiveness. The key is to approach them with patience and self-compassion, understanding that forgiveness is a process that takes time.

Mindfulness Exercises to Help Resolve Conflicts

Resolving conflicts is crucial in any relationship. Unresolved conflicts can decrease morale, cause communication breakdowns, and hinder the achievement of personal and shared goals. Addressing conflicts allows individuals to tackle underlying issues, improve communication skills, and foster mutual respect. By resolving conflicts promptly and effectively, unnecessary stress and tension can be avoided, helping to preserve the relationship. Mindfulness can be a powerful tool for resolving conflicts by promoting calm, empathy, and effective communication. Here are some mindfulness practices to help resolve conflicts constructively:

- **Mindful Breathing**: When a conflict arises, pause and take a few deep breaths. Inhale slowly through your nose, hold for a moment and exhale through your mouth. Focus on your breath to calm your mind and body, reducing immediate emotional reactivity. Practise this for a few minutes to regain composure before responding.
- **Active Listening:** Focus fully on the speaker, making eye contact and using non-verbal cues like nodding to show you are listening. Avoid interrupting or planning your response while the other person is speaking. Reflect on what you've heard to ensure understanding, such as

'It sounds like you're saying . . .' This practice helps you better understand the other person's perspective and reduces misunderstandings.

- **Empathy Practice:** After listening, take a moment to put yourself in the other person's shoes. Consider their feelings, needs, and perspectives without judgment. You might say, 'I can see how you might feel . . .' to express your understanding and validate their emotions. This practice fosters compassion and helps de-escalate tension.
- **Non-Judgmental Awareness:** Observe your thoughts and feelings about the conflict without labelling them as good or bad. Recognise your judgments or biases and acknowledge them without letting them dictate your responses. This approach helps you maintain a balanced perspective.
- **Mindful Reflection:** Reflect on your role in the conflict and your emotions. Ask yourself questions like, 'What is my contribution to this situation?' or 'How can I address my own triggers?' Use this insight to approach the conflict with greater self-awareness and responsibility.
- **Pause Before Reacting:** When you feel a strong emotional reaction, take a deliberate pause before responding. Use this time to breathe deeply and reflect on the best way to address the issue. A short pause helps prevent knee-jerk reactions and promotes more thoughtful, constructive responses.
- **Common Ground Finding:** Identify shared goals or values between you and the other person. Discuss these commonalities openly and use them as a foundation for finding mutually agreeable solutions. Focusing on shared interests helps build rapport and move towards resolution.
- **Expressing Feelings Mindfully:** When sharing your perspective, use 'I' statements to express how you feel

and what you need, such as 'I feel upset when . . .' or 'I need support with . . .' Avoid blaming or accusatory language, which can escalate conflict. This approach helps communicate your needs clearly while minimising defensiveness from the other party.

- **Mindful Problem-Solving:** Approach the conflict with a problem-solving mindset rather than focusing on personal grievances. Brainstorm potential solutions together, considering each person's needs and concerns. Evaluate the options collaboratively and agree on a solution that respects everyone's viewpoints.
- **Forgiveness Practice:** Reflect on the benefits of letting go of grudges and moving forward. Remember that forgiveness does not mean condoning negative behaviour but rather freeing yourself from ongoing resentment. Consider expressing forgiveness, either internally or directly, to help heal the relationship.

By incorporating these mindfulness practices, you can approach conflicts with greater calmness, empathy, and effectiveness, ultimately fostering healthier and more constructive resolutions.

Mindfulness Exercises to Overcome Grief

Grief is not just about the loss of an individual's life or presence; it also involves the disruption and alteration of relationships. Grief affects our interconnectedness with others, often triggering feelings of loneliness, abandonment, and disconnection. The death of a loved one brings intense emotions, such as sadness and longing, and can create a void in one's social network and support system. Unresolved conflicts or unspoken words within relationships can intensify feelings of regret and guilt after a loss. Therefore, when navigating grief, it is crucial to acknowledge the complex web of emotions that arise from varied relationships to heal and find meaningful ways to cope with the profound impact of loss on personal connections.

Mindfulness can be a powerful tool for coping with grief, helping you stay present with your emotions rather than becoming overwhelmed by them. Here are some mindfulness exercises designed to help process grief:

- **Breathing Meditation:** Sit or lie down in a comfortable position. Close your eyes and focus on your breath. Inhale deeply through your nose, hold for a moment, and exhale slowly through your mouth. Concentrate on the sensation of the air entering and leaving your body. This exercise helps ground you in the present moment, easing the anxiety or overwhelm that often accompanies grief.
- **Body Scan:** Starting at your feet, slowly bring your attention to each part of your body, noticing any sensations or tension. Gradually move up through your legs, torso, arms, and head. Take your time with each area, breathing into any discomfort you find. A body scan helps you become aware of where grief might be manifesting physically, allowing you to release tension and connect with your emotional state.
- **Mindful Walking:** Find a quiet place where you can walk slowly and without distraction. As you walk, focus on the sensation of your feet touching the ground, the movement of your legs, and the rhythm of your steps. Notice your surroundings—the sights, sounds, and smells. Mindful walking connects you to the present moment and your body, providing a break from the mental turmoil of grief.

- **Loving-Kindness Meditation:** Sit comfortably and take a few deep breaths. Begin by focusing on yourself and silently repeating phrases like 'May I be safe, may I be healthy, may I be at peace.' Then, extend these wishes to others, including the person you're grieving, and finally to all beings. This meditation cultivates compassion and helps you process difficult emotions, fostering a sense of peace and acceptance.
- **Grief Journalling:** Set aside time to write about your grief without judgment. Start by describing how you feel in the present moment. You can also write letters to the person you've lost, expressing things you wish you could have said or done. Writing can be a form of mindfulness, allowing you to explore and express your emotions in a safe, contained way.
- **Mindful Visualisation:** Close your eyes and visualise a place where you feel safe and at peace. It could be a real place you know or an imagined one. Spend a few minutes mentally exploring this space, noticing details, and allowing yourself to feel calm and protected. Visualisation provides a mental escape, offering a reprieve from the intensity of grief while reinforcing a sense of safety and well-being.
- **Emotional Awareness Meditation:** Sit quietly and bring your awareness to any emotions you are experiencing. Allow yourself to feel them fully without trying to change them. Label the emotions (e.g., sadness, anger, confusion) and observe how they move and change within you. This practice helps you stay with your grief without becoming overwhelmed, allowing the emotions to pass through you naturally.
- **Practise Mindful Gratitude**: Reflect on things or moments you are grateful for, even during your grief. This could include positive memories with the person

you lost, support from loved ones, or simple things like the warmth of the sun. Gratitude practice doesn't negate grief but can help balance it, reminding you of the good that still exists in your life.

Each of these exercises can be adjusted to fit your comfort level and needs. The key is to approach them with gentle curiosity and kindness, allowing yourself to be exactly where you are in your grief journey.

Mindfulness Practices as a Morning Ritual

Establishing a consistent morning routine can significantly boost productivity, focus, and overall well-being. By starting each day with intentional rituals—such as exercise, meditation, planning daily tasks, and eating a nutritious breakfast—you can cultivate a sense of discipline and control. This structure helps you prioritise tasks effectively, reduce stress levels, and enhance decision-making skills.

Morning rituals offer an opportunity for self-care and reflection, enabling you to start the day on a positive note and better handle the challenges that may arise.

Below is a simple mindfulness activity to try as soon as you wake up, before checking your phone or starting your day:

- **Set the Scene:** Find a comfortable spot near an open window, where fresh air can gently blow on your face, and sit quietly.
- **Begin with Deep Breathing:** Close your eyes and take three slow, deep breaths. Inhale deeply through your nose, hold for a moment, and exhale slowly through your mouth. Focus on the sensation of the breath entering and leaving your body.

- **Engage Your Senses:** Use the 5-4-3-2-1 method to fully engage your senses, leading to a deep sense of gratitude.
  - o 5 Things You Can See: Open your eyes and look around your space. Notice five things in your environment. Carefully observe each one, taking in the colours, shapes, and details you might usually overlook.
  - o 4 Things You Can Feel: Close your eyes again and focus on touch. Notice four different sensations, such as the feel of your sheets, the temperature of the air, the texture of your clothing, or the pressure of your body against the bed or chair.
  - o 3 Things You Can Hear: Listen for three distinct sounds, such as the distant hum of traffic, birds chirping, or the sound of your own breathing. Listen without trying to change or judge the sounds.
  - o 2 Things You Can Smell: Notice two different smells in your environment. It could be the scent of your room, fresh air coming through the window, or the aroma of your morning coffee or tea if it's brewing nearby.
  - o 1 Thing You Can Taste: Focus on your sense of taste. If you haven't eaten yet, notice the residual taste in your mouth, or take a sip of water or tea and fully experience the flavour.
- **Set an Intention for the Day:** After grounding yourself in your senses, take a moment to set a positive intention for the day. It could be a simple affirmation like 'I will approach today with calm and clarity' or a specific goal like 'I will be patient and kind in my interactions.'
- **Close with Gratitude:** End your practice by thinking of one thing you're grateful for. It could be something simple, like the comfort of your bed or the opportunity

to start a new day. Allow yourself to fully appreciate this feeling of gratitude.

This ritual, taking just a few minutes each morning, can help you start your day with a clear mind, a centred heart, and a sense of purpose.

Mindfulness Practices as a Bedtime Ritual

Rituals before bedtime are essential for establishing a sense of routine and stability, particularly for children. These rituals signal to the body and mind that it is time to wind down and prepare for rest, aiding in the development of healthy sleep patterns. Calming activities such as reading, taking a warm bath, or practising mindfulness exercises can lower stress levels and alleviate anxiety, promoting relaxation before bed.

- **Bathe in Lukewarm Water:** Take a bath in lukewarm water and moisturise your body afterwards.
- **Jal Neti:** Cleanse your nostrils using the Jal Neti procedure. Brushing your teeth and ensuring your mouth is free of any food particles is essential.
- **Massage Feet with Castor Oil:** Massage the soles of your feet and between your toes with a small amount of castor oil. This nourishes tired feet after a long day.
- **Put the Phone Away:** Place your phone out of reach to avoid distractions before and during sleep.
- **Mindful Breathing:** Sit or lie in a comfortable position. Close your eyes and take slow, deep breaths. Inhale through your nose, allowing your belly to rise, and exhale slowly through your mouth. Focus on the sensation of your breath. If your mind wanders, gently bring your attention back to your breathing.

- **Body Scan Meditation:** Lie on your back with your arms at your sides. Begin by focusing on your toes and noticing any sensations. Gradually move your attention up your body—feet, legs, torso, arms, neck, and head. At each point, observe any tension or discomfort, and consciously release it as you exhale.
- **Progressive Muscle Relaxation:** While lying down, start by tensing the muscles in your feet, holding for a few seconds, and then releasing. Gradually move up your body, tensing and relaxing each muscle group—calves, thighs, abdomen, chest, arms, shoulders, neck, and face.
- **Visualisation:** Close your eyes and imagine a peaceful place—a beach, forest, or any environment where you feel calm and safe. Engage all your senses: hear the sounds, feel the textures, notice the colours, and take in the smells. Spend a few minutes immersed in this scene.
- **Mindful Gratitude:** Before bed, think of three things you are grateful for. Reflect on why you are grateful, allowing yourself to fully experience the associated emotions. You can do this mentally or write them in a journal.
- **Mindful Listening:** Sit quietly in your bedroom with your eyes closed. Listen attentively to the sounds around you—the hum of the fan, distant traffic, or the rustling of sheets. Focus on each sound without trying to identify or judge it.
- **Loving-Kindness Meditation:** Sit or lie comfortably, and bring to mind someone you care about. Silently repeat phrases like 'May you be happy, may you be healthy, may you be peaceful.' After a few minutes, extend these wishes to yourself, and then to others, including neutral or challenging people.
- **Mindful Stretching:** Perform gentle stretches before bed, focusing on the sensations in your muscles and joints. Stretch your arms, legs, neck, and back, holding

each stretch for a few deep breaths. Pay attention to how your body feels in each position.

Integrating one or more of these mindfulness exercises into your bedtime routine can help you transition into a state of relaxation and enhance the quality of your sleep.

Mindfulness Exercises to Practise as a Family

Performing routines together as a family is crucial for fostering a sense of unity, structure, and connection within the household. Families can strengthen their bonds and enhance communication by engaging in consistent family routines, such as sharing meals, participating in recreational activities, or attending religious services. These shared experiences create opportunities for open dialogue, problem-solving, and traditions that build resilience during challenging times. Additionally, engaging in routines together instils a sense of responsibility and accountability among family members, promoting cooperation and mutual respect. Families that practise regular routines experience lower levels of stress and anxiety, improved well-being, and higher levels of satisfaction with family life.

Here are some mindfulness exercises that can be enjoyable and beneficial for the whole family:

- **Mindful Breathing Together:** Sit in a circle with your family—either on the floor or chairs. Close your eyes or maintain a soft gaze and take a few deep breaths. Encourage everyone to focus on their breath, noticing the sensation of the air entering and leaving their bodies. You can synchronise your breathing by inhaling and exhaling together or breathe at your own pace. Do this for 3–5 minutes, then take a moment to share how everyone feels.

- **Gratitude Circle:** Sit together in a comfortable space. Each family member takes a turn sharing one thing they are grateful for that day. Encourage everyone to listen mindfully, without interrupting or judging. Continue around the circle for a few rounds, allowing everyone to express gratitude. This practice helps foster a positive atmosphere and strengthens connections.
- **Mindful Eating as a Family:** During a meal, invite everyone to take a moment to appreciate the food before eating. Encourage each person to notice the colours, textures, and smells of the food on their plate. Take the first few bites slowly, savouring the taste and texture. As you eat, discuss the experience together—what does the food taste like? How does it make you feel? This exercise helps everyone appreciate the meal and promotes mindful eating habits.
- **Family Nature Walk:** Go for a walk together in nature, whether it's a park, forest, or your neighbourhood. As you walk, encourage everyone to be fully present, noticing the sights, sounds, and smells around them. Ask each person to point out something they find interesting or beautiful along the way. You can also practise mindful listening by pausing to hear the sounds of nature, like birds singing or leaves rustling. This activity promotes mindfulness while enjoying quality time outdoors.
- **Mindful Storytelling:** Gather the family for a storytelling session, where each person shares a story or memory. As each person speaks, the rest of the family listens mindfully, without interrupting. After the story is told, you can discuss what you learnt from the story or how it made you feel. This practice encourages mindful listening, creativity, and sharing.

- **Mindful Art:** Set up a space with art supplies like paper, markers, crayons, or paint. Encourage everyone to create a drawing or painting mindfully, focusing on the process rather than the outcome. As you draw or paint, pay attention to the colours, shapes, and movements of your hands. Afterwards, share your artwork with the family and talk about the experience. This exercise promotes mindfulness, creativity, and self-expression.
- **Mindful Bedtime Routine:** Before bedtime, gather for a short and calming mindfulness practice. You can practise deep breathing, listen to a guided meditation, or do a simple body scan where you relax each part of your body. Encourage everyone to let go of the day's stress and focus on relaxing their minds and bodies. This routine can help create a peaceful transition to sleep and improve the quality of rest for everyone.
- **Mindful Listening Games:** Play a game where each person takes turns being the speaker and the listener. The speaker shares something, such as what they enjoyed most about their day, while the listener pays full attention without interrupting. After the speaker finishes, the listener reflects on what they heard, ensuring they understood correctly. This game helps improve communication skills and fosters mindful listening.
- **Mindful Body Movement:** Choose a simple yoga or stretching routine that the whole family can do together. As you move through each pose or stretch, encourage everyone to pay attention to their bodies—how does each movement feel? Focus on breathing deeply and moving slowly, maintaining awareness of the present moment. You can also try a mindful dance session where everyone moves freely to music, focusing on the joy of movement. This exercise promotes physical awareness, relaxation, and fun.

- **Mindful Breathing with a Stuffed Animal (for Younger Children):** Have each child lie down with a stuffed animal on their belly. Ask them to take slow, deep breaths and watch the stuffed animal rise and fall with each breath. This helps them focus on their breathing in a simple, visual way. It's a calming practice that can help younger children develop mindfulness skills.

These mindfulness exercises can help your family build stronger connections, reduce stress, and cultivate a more mindful, present lifestyle together.

This book intends to equip both myself and my readers with coping skills for facing adversities. Mindfulness does not mean staying calm all the time or having answers to every uncomfortable situation we encounter in life. Practising mindfulness helps us become more aware of how blessed we are, identify solutions to our problems, and determine the best way to cope with challenges given the circumstances. I sincerely hope that this chapter and this book serve as a helpful reference for overcoming life's hiccups.

Embracing Authenticity through Mindfulness

'The privilege of a lifetime is to become who you truly are.'

—Carl Jung

The book you just finished reading delves into my journey into mindfulness. This serendipitous exploration began as a response to an existential crisis I experienced a few years before the pandemic. Questions about my identity, purpose, relationships, and the nature of existence plagued my mind. These inquiries continue to linger, prompting me to seek answers. While I may not have all the solutions I seek, I have discovered a fundamental truth that I believe will guide me and future generations—that of authenticity.

Authenticity has been the most significant revelation on my mindfulness journey. When our thoughts and actions align with our emotions and actions, we experience a profound sense of contentment. Mindfulness enables us to become more self-aware of our thoughts, actions, and emotions, allowing us to make necessary adjustments to maintain harmony. This process may involve accepting ourselves as we are and acknowledging that we are enough.

Embracing authenticity may require stepping out of our comfort zones, breaking generational patterns, or simply learning to say no. In today's fast-paced world, it is easy to lose touch with ourselves amidst the demands of daily life. However, by integrating mindfulness and authenticity into our routines, we can cultivate a deeper understanding of ourselves and foster self-acceptance. By aligning our actions with our core values, we can lead more purposeful lives and find greater fulfilment.

Who am I? I often wondered,
Not something new
Not something new
I tell myself ever so often to assuage those emotions few.

I remember those days crystal clear
I remember them as though they were still near
I was corrected by mom's family for speaking a lingo that belonged to my dad's
And my dad's family thought my turning vegetarian was just a fad.

Who am I? I often wondered . . .
I thought it didn't matter as I was just trying to adapt.
I thought it didn't matter as that was the norm in fact.

Fast forward and I got married into a family very different from mine.
Language and caste no bar, was said
Phew that's a relief, I thought, don't have to now haggle with the confused heads
Planning of budgets, no spicy food and no importance to dressing!
I don't even know how that works, you've got to be kidding!
I changed, I managed, I became a person anew
For it was important for me and him and ours, too.

Who am I? I often wondered . . .
I thought it didn't matter as I was just trying to adapt.
I thought it didn't matter as that was the norm in fact.

Global trotters we became, leaving no stone unturned,
To ensure our little one could become a beautiful human with experiences well-earned
Nomads we became with no place to call our own,
Except the passport that states otherwise and the place where we were born.

Who am I? I often wondered . . .
I thought it didn't matter as I was just trying to adapt.
I thought it didn't matter as that was the norm in fact.

Trips back home earlier always used to be fun
Shopping, meeting family, and lots of sun.
Tears, laughter, misunderstandings, and memories were made.
All that was packed into the two weeks
And off we went back to our home that our hearts used to seek.

Each time around I felt different
When emotions were stoked
And as families grew and apart
Expanding the gaps and making home more distant
And tugging every time at my heart

Who am I? I often wondered . . .
I thought it didn't matter as I was just trying to adapt.
I thought it didn't matter as that was the norm in fact.

Sometimes I feel I've never left the shores of who I am
Sometimes it feels like the boat has sailed and I've moved on.
I soon realise this is just the path of progress
Challenges are but a reminder so I don't digress
We are not who we used to be with the passage of time.
But then why and how could we be after the uphill climb?

So, who am I? I dare again ask
When I fail to understand this impact,
Communication becomes a task
Is this really me or am I hiding behind a mask?

I adapted, I changed for the better me
Things are clearer than they used to be
I am who the present of me requires
I am the one who is adept at fighting fires
I am also the one who is full of acceptance
Of my past, my present and in that there is no question.

The individual in him and her and all others
Defines their ask of me and my perimeters
For at the end, the cross they bear on their own,
These relationships are but those that we have sown.

We change, we adapt, and we own who we are.
For the rest are taken, and there has been only one me this far.

—Aatmanika Ram

Acknowledgements

Gratitude is a word that I use a lot these days. I express my gratitude for every contribution to a pleasant and memorable experience—people, opportunities, availability of resources, and above all, good health. However, there are some things I am eternally grateful for—things that have enabled good experiences and contributed to mitigating the not-so-good ones in my life.

I would like to express my heartfelt gratitude to my mother, Shrimati Subashini, who previously served as the editor-in-chief of *Gnanabhumi*, a prominent Hindu religious magazine. Your blessings are invaluable to me, and I am confident that your wisdom will continue to illuminate the path for future generations. Your unwavering faith in the divine is a perpetual source of inspiration, and your knack for problem-solving has taught me that there is always a silver lining.

I am also deeply appreciative of my father, Shri T. G. Somasundaram, who has instilled the ability to create something extraordinary out of nothing in me. His tireless dedication to providing for our family's needs, including food, clothing, and education—against all odds—is a gift for which I am eternally grateful.

I would also like to express a deep gratitude to my aunts, Veda Rangan and (late) Saroja Sundararajan, who have been a great source of inspiration in many of the endeavours that I take on today. Veda Rangan is a living truth who embodies, strength, willpower, and resilience and has shown infinite ability to face challenges head-on. Her generosity of time and resources knows no bounds, and I can only hope to remember her teaching in the face of adversity. My other aunt, (late) Saroja Sundararajan has been a mentor to me in several ways—whether it was helping me with my thesis during my master's or teaching me the nuances of cooking, she was there for me, upfront and centre. I miss her but I also know I have her blessings.

I must also acknowledge (late) Professor M. V. Hariharan and Smt. Malathi Hariharan, my esteemed in-laws, for their unwavering support in all my endeavours. Their encouragement and non-interfering nature have provided me with the energy to strive further.

To my esteemed readers, I am truly humbled by the positive impact my last book has had on many of you. Your feedback and comments have been incredibly inspiring, and I am grateful for each one of them. Your unwavering support has played a crucial role in the creation of *Ancient Practices for Mindful Living*.

I am committed to assisting my readers in overcoming challenges and achieving personal growth through the wisdom shared in this book. Thank you for your continued support and encouragement.

I extend my heartfelt gratitude to my dear friend Barathy Shankar for her unwavering support during the challenging and joyful moments of my life. Her encouragement to explore counselling and Cognitive Behavioural Therapy (CBT) as a path to healing has been invaluable. Her guidance has helped me view therapy not as a taboo but as a constructive tool for personal growth and well-being.

I would like to express my appreciation to Dr Aravind for meticulously reviewing every word I have written related to medical science and providing valuable insights.

I am thankful to Chitra Sukumar for introducing me to guided meditation in a gentle manner and for being a true source of inspiration in ways that she never thought she would be. A special mention goes to Viji Shivaram for her remarkable memory of happy moments, always ready to uplift my spirits in times of need. Sincere thanks to Vidya Babu for being the ever-so-kind person and the most important connection to my happy childhood memories.

I am thankful for the guidance and support I have received from my yoga teacher, Raksha Agarwal, a student of Dev Sanskriti Vishwavidyalaya University, Haridwar. She has provided me with effective solutions to alleviate physical discomfort through appropriate asanas and emphasising the importance of breath work in emotional regulation. I am also very thankful to her for sharing information with me based on extensive research done at the university.

I am also grateful to Malini Raghavan for her unwavering patience and non-judgmental attitude whenever I needed someone to confide in. Her calm presence and empathetic listening have had a profound calming effect on me—perhaps more than she realises.

I would like to express my deepest gratitude to my husband, Ramani Hariharan, and our daughter, Sanghamithra Ramani, for their unwavering support and patience. Despite my constant reminders to myself about the importance of having my own identity beyond being known as Ramani's wife and Sanghamithra's mother, I cannot deny that there is nothing in this world that brings me greater joy. Both of you inspire me to be a better person each day, and for that I am truly grateful.

I am grateful to everyone with whom I have crossed paths and for enriching my understanding of living life to the fullest. Your presence has helped me realise that every moment is precious and worth cherishing.

I am also thankful for all the amazing experiences with those who are no longer part of my life. The memories we created during good times in our lives fill me with warmth even today. Your absence rings very loud at times, but I do know that every experience carries a lesson. I thank you for leaving my life, for it is then that I realised strengths in me that I never knew I had, weaknesses in me that I knew I must work on to heal myself, and above all, generational cycles that I need to break so that my child never feels the loss.

I am truly blessed to have such remarkable individuals in my life, whose guidance and support have shaped me into the person I am today.